U N D E R S T A N D I N G
T H E
BOOK OF MORMON

UNDERSTANDING THE
BOOK OF MORMON

A Quick Christian Guide to the Mormon Holy Book

ROSS ANDERSON

ZONDERVAN.com/
AUTHORTRACKER
follow your favorite authors

ZONDERVAN

Understanding the Book of Mormon
Copyright © 2009 by Ross Anderson

Requests for information should be addressed to:

Zondervan, *Grand Rapids, Michigan 49530*

Library of Congress Cataloging-in-Publication Data

Anderson, Ross, 1955 –
    Understanding the book of Mormon : A quick Christian guide to the Mormon holy book/ Ross J. Anderson.
        p. cm.
    Includes bibliographical references and indexes.
    ISBN 978-0-310-28321-8 (softcover, gate fold)
    1. Book of Mormon — Criticism, interpretation, etc. I. Title.
BX8627.A675 2008
289.3'22 — dc22   2008021320

Any Internet addresses (websites, blogs, etc.) and telephone numbers printed in this book are offered as a resource. They are not intended in any way to be or imply an endorsement by Zondervan, nor does Zondervan vouch for the content of these sites and numbers for the life of this book.

Interior design by Melissa Elenbaas

Printed in the United States of America

09 10 11 12 13 14 • 23 22 21 20 19 18 17 16 15 14 13 12 11 10 9 8 7 6 5 4 3 2 1

CONTENTS

120286

PREFACE

This book has been written both to explain and to evaluate the Book of Mormon from the perspective of the historic Christian faith. My intention is to interact with Mormonism in a spirit of kindness and civility. Thus, I submitted the most controversial chapters to faithful Latter-day Saints for critique, who, along with others, have helped me to avoid words that might seem contemptuous or argumentative. My intention is to present LDS views with accuracy and fairness and to represent Mormonism as it is currently believed and practiced. Along with my own experience growing up Mormon and leading a church in Utah for many years, I have also read broadly from both popular and scholarly LDS literature. Again, my LDS readers have given me invaluable feedback to help me present their views correctly.

Some evangelical readers may be disappointed that this book is not more forceful. While I state good reasons for rejecting LDS claims about the Book of Mormon, my purpose is not to triumph in a battle of words. I hope to provide insight about the subject, but also to model a way of interacting with others that speaks the truth in love, with gentleness and respect. Ironically, Latter-day Saints will probably view this as an "anti-Mormon" book despite my efforts to be fair and kind, simply because I have not agreed with them.

This book is, by necessity, limited in its depth. Much more could be written to explain and support both LDS and traditional Christian views. Yet as an introduction, its role is not to develop every point or to cover every related subject. Thus I have provided ample footnotes to establish the credibility of my position as well as to direct interested readers to sources that discuss the issues in greater detail.

While the Church of Jesus Christ of Latter-day Saints is commonly known as the Mormon Church, Latter-day Saints prefer the official title. This is cumbersome for the writer and the reader. Their preferred abbreviation is "The Church of Jesus Christ." Yet in my mind, this implies an exclusive status that I cannot grant. As an alternative, I will refer to "the LDS Church" in most cases. At times, I will use the terms "Mormon" and "LDS" as adjectives to refer to the church and to elements of the culture that it creates. I will also use "Mormon" as a noun to refer to the people themselves. Some Latter-day Saints see this term as promoting negative stereotypes about them. My motive is not to label or marginalize Latter-day Saints but simply to provide stylistic variation. Moreover, the use of the term by the LDS Church itself supports the validity of my decision.

Typically, Bible verses are taken from the New International Version. When the Bible is quoted from the Mormon perspective, I use the King James Version (the official version of the LDS Church) as a way of putting the reader into the Latter-day Saint's shoes.

I am deeply grateful to family members and friends who have given input, especially those who took time to critique the manuscript, and to my spiritual family at Wasatch Evangelical Free Church for their patience and gracious support. I am also thankful to the excellent staff at Zondervan for their help. While I have received many valuable suggestions from trusted friends, I alone am responsible for the book's shortcomings.

1

THE GOLD BIBLE

What Is the Book of Mormon?

As a teenager, it wasn't easy getting up at 6:00 a.m. to start the school day. I've never been a morning person, but every day at daybreak, before heading to my first period class at Tustin High, I went to the chapel of the Church of Jesus Christ of Latter-day Saints to attend a class on the Book of Mormon. During four years of early morning studies, we learned about other topics as well.

Growing up in an active LDS home, the Book of Mormon held a prominent place in my family's life. We admired its heroes and quoted from its inspiring passages. We modeled our actions on its stories and principles. Above all, the Book of Mormon verified everything we believed. We were convinced that Joseph Smith had received it from God and translated it by divine power. So for my family—as for Latter-day Saints today—the very existence of the Book of Mormon proved that Smith was God's prophet for our times and that the Church he founded was true.

Mormonism in the Spotlight

Since my teen years, the influence of Mormonism in American life has grown. Most people have seen clean-cut Mormon missionaries riding their bicycles through the streets. Television commercials highlight LDS family virtues. Internet pop-up ads promise to answer our deepest questions about life. *Newsweek* magazine featured a cover story on "The

Mormons" just before the 2002 Winter Olympics, which showcased the Mormon heartland of Salt Lake City. Gordon B. Hinckley, as President of the LDS Church, was interviewed in *Time* magazine and on *Larry King Live*.

Mormonism appears frequently on the radar of popular culture through sports and entertainment figures like football Hall of Famer Steve Young, country music trio SheDaisy, R & B legend Gladys Knight, and comic actor Jon Heder. Likewise, Latter-day Saints make their mark in the highest levels of government, from Senate Majority Leader Harry Reid of Nevada to Michael Leavitt, Secretary of Health and Human Services. Of course, nothing has focused America's attention on Mormonism more than Mitt Romney's 2008 presidential campaign.

But despite its expanding profile, myths and misconceptions about Mormonism abound. In public, LDS spokesmen downplay their Church's distinctive doctrines. Christian writers often recycle archaic and inaccurate portrayals of Mormon beliefs. The popular media focus on stereotypes of polygamy or the perceived quirks of LDS culture. Thus the story and message of the Book of Mormon are largely unknown to most Americans—despite its position as the central scripture of this growing faith and a powerful defining force in Mormon life. By 2001, the Book of Mormon was available in ninety-nine different languages. It is the second most widely distributed religious book in America—trailing only the Bible. More than 100 million copies have been printed, with over fifteen thousand added every day.[1] Yet even informed Christians generally know little about the Book of Mormon.

The Astonishing Claims of the Book of Mormon

Latter-day Saints make some remarkable assertions about their foundational scripture. According to the LDS Church, the Book of Mormon is "a collection of writings and teachings of the ancient prophets and followers of Jesus Christ who lived in the Americas from approximately 590 BC to AD 421. The Prophet Joseph Smith translated the Book of Mormon by divine inspiration from gold plates that he received from the angel Moroni."[2]

Joseph Smith studies the gold plates.

To begin with, the Book of Mormon is presented as an ancient account of the inhabitants of America — people who are considered to be descendants of Israel and "the principal ancestors of the American Indians."[3] The Book of Mormon claims to be an abridgment of their records, engraved on plates of gold and buried in the ground for posterity. Thus to Latter-day Saints, the book does not merely tell a faith-promoting story, nor is it a simple chronology. It is a spiritual history comparable to the Bible: the story of God's people in the Americas, their response to God's prophets, and their cycles of wickedness and repentance. As spiritual history, the highlight of the Book of Mormon's plot is the appearance of Jesus Christ himself in America.

The Book of Mormon makes the further claim that the gold plates containing this ancient record "were delivered to Joseph Smith, who translated them by the gift and power of God."[4] The plates were said to be inscribed in a script called "reformed Egyptian."[5] Smith did not translate these engraved characters in a strict sense. Rather, Mormons believe that God showed him by supernatural means what the archaic words meant in English. Smith then dictated this "translation" to a scribe. Completed in just a few months, the Book of Mormon was published in 1830 in Palmyra, New York.

In the earliest years of Mormonism, it was known by proponents and detractors alike as the "Gold Bible." Certainly its language is reminiscent of and draws heavily from the Bible. But this title reflects its most fundamental claim: that the Book of Mormon, like the Bible, is the Word of God.

"A Marvelous Work and a Wonder"

Another assertion made about the Book of Mormon has to do with its grand significance in God's plan. The appearance of the Book of Mormon is seen by Latter-day Saints as a great work of God ushering in the final era of history. Mormonism teaches that the original Church founded by Jesus fell into apostasy. Foundational truths were lost and confused. The organization and authority established by Jesus were forfeited. As a result, God chose Joseph Smith as a prophet to restore original Christianity. The appearance of the Book of Mormon serves as a harbinger of this restoration and of Christ's subsequent return to earth. For example, when God predicts: "Therefore, behold, I will proceed to do a marvellous work among this people, even a marvellous work and a wonder" (Isaiah 29:14 KJV), Latter-day Saints believe that the Book of Mormon is in view.

It follows, then, that claims for the Book of Mormon are intertwined with claims about Joseph Smith. The book's introduction asserts that "those who gain a testimony of its truth and divinity" will also gain the knowledge from God "that Joseph Smith is his revelator and prophet in these last days, and The Church of Jesus Christ of Latter-day Saints is the Lord's kingdom once again established on the earth."[6] Thus the Book of Mormon functions as a sign validating Smith and his work. If the Book of Mormon is true, then Smith is God's appointed prophet and the Church he founded is the only true agent of God's kingdom. In fact, the LDS strategy for gaining converts is to urge people to read the Book of Mormon and pray for a personal revelation from God. This positive inner feeling constitutes the person's "testimony of its truth and divinity." For that individual, the experience authenticates the divine origin of the Book of Mormon and everything the book represents.

Joseph Smith

Joseph Smith certainly claimed an exalted status for the Book of Mormon. In his journal he once wrote: "I told the brethren that the Book of Mormon was the most correct of any book on earth, and the keystone of our religion, and a man would get nearer to God by abiding by its precepts, than by any other book."[7] In Smith's account of how he received the Book of Mormon, he claimed that an angel appeared to him one night.

> He said there was a book deposited, written upon gold plates, giving an account of the former inhabitants of this continent, and the source from which they sprang. He also said that the fulness of the everlasting Gospel was contained in it, as delivered by the Savior to the ancient inhabitants.[8]

To outsiders, it seems extravagant to assert that this book is the most accurate or truthful on Earth, that it trumps all others in spiritual value, or that it contains "the fulness of the everlasting Gospel." Claims like this explain why opinions about the Book of Mormon are so polarized. The book itself leaves little room for middle ground.

A Controversial Book

Since my teenage years, I have changed my opinion about the Book of Mormon. As a young adult, I discovered a wide spectrum of views about this unique book. When it was first published, newspapers near Joseph Smith's home treated it as a contemptible superstition. Others have seen the book as the product of Smith's religious imagination. Perhaps the most famous and colorful critique of the Book of Mormon comes from Mark Twain, who called it "chloroform in print."[9] In 1831, Alexander Campbell wrote a critique of the Book of Mormon denying any inspired origin: "This prophet Smith, through his stone spectacles, wrote on the plates of Nephi, in his book of Mormon, every error and almost every truth discussed in N. York for the last ten years."[10] Critics see the Book of Mormon as a pious fraud reflecting nineteenth-century America rather than any ancient civilization, or as the result of some mystical or psychological experience.

Nevertheless, many early readers found something compelling about the Book of Mormon. Parley P. Pratt wrote: "As I read, the spirit of the Lord was upon me, and I knew and comprehended that the book was true.... This discovery enlarged my heart, and filled my soul with joy and gladness."[11] To faithful Latter-day Saints, now as then, it seems impossible that a rustic, semiliterate farm boy living in the 1820s could have produced the Book of Mormon without divine power. To them, it can only be an authentic ancient scripture of great spiritual significance. A Mormon leader recently bore witness that "the Book of Mormon is one of the greatest sources of spiritual power given to men and women on earth to guide us on our quest for eternal life."[12]

Can Twelve Million People Be Wrong?

Believing the Book of Mormon to be from God, millions of Latter-day Saints read the book diligently. They use it to train their children in moral and spiritual principles. They seek to live its ideals. Mormon scholars vigorously advocate reasons to accept the Book of Mormon as ancient scripture on par with the Bible. Most of the thousands of people who convert to Mormonism each year claim a special experience of divine revelation upon reading the Book of Mormon. They gain a compelling testimony of its truth and thus of the truth of the LDS Church. As a result, former LDS Church President Gordon B. Hinckley said: "I cannot understand why the Christian world does not accept this book."[13]

What is the basis for these beliefs and practices? Why does historic, biblical Christianity deny a divine origin for the Book of Mormon? As we begin to evaluate this exceptional book and the claims associated with it, let's start by taking a closer look at the basic story the Book of Mormon tells.

2

A TALE OF TWO CIVILIZATIONS

What Is the Book of Mormon About?

For seven nights each summer, a hillside near Palmyra, New York, is transformed into a massive, ten-level outdoor stage. A cast of over 650 people, dressed in exotic costumes and supported by a high-tech music and light show, presents an epic drama for over sixty thousand onlookers. The performance is full of action and adventure involving the heroes and villains of two competing civilizations. For over fifty years, the Hill Cumorah Pageant has stirred the imagination of Latter-day Saints by reenacting the story of the Book of Mormon.

Mormons believe the Book of Mormon describes the civilizations that inhabited America during ancient times. The grand tale covers a span of over one thousand years, with a side story stretching back centuries more. Claiming to be ancient scripture, the Book of Mormon is a collection of fifteen books, each named after its original author and divided by chapter and verse. Authors of these books include generals, prophets, and kings. They wrote sermons, battle stories, poetry, travelogues, religious and political commentary, and more. The care of these ancient records, inscribed on metal tablets, was handed down, usually from father to son. According to the Book of Mormon timeline, in about AD 385 a prophet named Mormon abridged these extensive records onto a single set of gold plates. His son Moroni buried the plates in the hill called Cumorah to preserve them for the future.

Lehi and His Family

The Book of Mormon story opens around 600 BC in Jerusalem. A Jewish prophet named Lehi had a vision warning him that the city would soon be destroyed. But when the people rejected his message of repentance, Lehi led his family and a few others into the wilderness. Lehi's older sons, Laman and Lemuel, unwilling to abandon the family's comfortable life, resisted their father. By contrast, his youngest son, Nephi, desired to obey God and became the group's spiritual leader. In the wilderness, God told Nephi that his family would be led to a land of promise, "choice above all other lands" (1 Nephi 2:20).

Lehi's party spent nearly ten years wandering the Arabian Desert, guided by a miraculous compass called the Liahona. Based on the faith and diligence of the user, the Liahona pointed in the correct direction of travel. At times, words appeared around its edges to give guidance about God's ways.

The Liahona

By Steven Henry. Commissioned by the author.

Conflict between Lehi's sons erupted often during the journey. For instance, while sailing to the promised land, Laman and Lemuel rebelled against Nephi and tied him up. As a result, the Liahona stopped working. In serious peril from a fierce storm and ignorant of where to steer the ship, the brothers relented. As Nephi prayed, the storm subsided and the families safely concluded their journey.

When the travelers reached America, they planted crops and raised flocks. But because of his brothers' animosity, Nephi and his followers soon parted from Laman and Lemuel to start over in a new region, where the people made Nephi their king.

Nephites, Lamanites, and Other -Ites

The two clans that arose from Lehi's family became two rival societies that developed along divergent paths. The Book of Mormon describes the Nephites as industrious. They built buildings, including a temple modeled after the one in Jerusalem, where they practiced the Judaism of their fathers. They developed metallurgy and produced weapons. They raised various kinds of grain and fruit and kept flocks of cattle, goats, and horses. The Nephites were governed first by kings and later by elected judges. They remained literate and kept written records. The Book of Mormon is narrated largely from a Nephite perspective, as it claims to be a part of those records.

By contrast, the Lamanites are described as "a lazy and an idolatrous people" (Mosiah 9:12), "wild, ferocious and bloodthirsty" (Enos 1:20), "an idle people, full of mischief and subtlety" (2 Nephi 5:24), whose economy was based on hunting and on raiding the hated Nephites. Having rejected God's commandments, the Lamanites were cursed with a dark skin and degenerated into barbarism and savagery.

Many of the Book of Mormon's heroic stories involve righteous Nephites trying to convert the Lamanites from idolatry. At one point, Lamanite King Lamoni was miraculously converted through the wisdom and courage of Ammon, a Nephite missionary. The king then led many of his people to faith. One passage describes what happened when Lamanites were thus rehabilitated:

> Therefore, all the Lamanites who had become converted unto the Lord did unite with their brethren.... And their curse was taken from them, and their skin became white like unto the Nephites. And their young men and their daughters became exceedingly fair, and they were numbered among the Nephites, and were called Nephites. (3 Nephi 2:12, 15)

In other words, what began as a separation between two Jewish clans eventually became a political, cultural, and even a spiritual division. Through the course of the story, various groups of dissenters left the Nephites and joined with the Lamanites. When Lamanites were converted, they came to be called Nephites.

BOOKS OF THE BOOK OF MORMON			
Book	Synopsis	Chapters	Time Frame
1 Nephi	The migration of Lehi's family from Jerusalem through Arabia to America.	22	600–570 BC
2 Nephi	Division into two nations after Lehi's death. Doctrinal discourses of Lehi and Nephi.	33	570–544 BC
Jacob	After the first generation, the people begin to fall away from truth. Doctrinal discourse.	7	After 544 BC

Enos	Social and spiritual conditions among Nephites and Lamanites.	1	To 420 BC
Jarom	Economic and military success of Nephites for several decades due to their obedience of God.	1	399–361 BC
Omni	Cycles of war and peace for generations. Discovery of Mulekite kingdom of Zarahemla and their merger with the Nephites.	1	360–130 BC
Words of Mormon	The ancient editor, Mormon, inserts an explanation of his sources and the history of the records he abridged.	1	AD 385
Mosiah	The Nephites divide and migrate to new lands. Their wars. Discovery of Jaredites. Prophetic preaching leads to renewal of true religion. Some Nephite groups join the Lamanites, while others are reunited to the main Nephite body.	29	200–91 BC

Alma	Change from monarchy to the rule of judges. Political turmoil among the Nephites. Threats from Lamanite armies and from political coups. Much preaching to Nephites and Lamanites. Many Lamanites converted and join the Nephites	63	91–53 BC
Hela-man	Conditions grow better, then worse in Nephite society. Continued wars and political chaos. Warlords control Nephite government. Righteous Lamanites urge the Nephites to repent.	16	52–1 BC
3 Nephi	Signs announce the birth of Christ. Nephites survive war only to become prosperous, proud, and hard-hearted. Christ appears, bringing great destruction upon the land. He teaches his followers and sets up his church.	30	AD 1–35
4 Nephi	200 years of unity, peace, and justice follow Christ's advent. In another 100 years, the people revert to old divisions and evils.	1	AD 36–321

Mor-mon	The Nephites grow more wicked than the Lamanites. Massive wars ensue, until the Nephites are completely annihilated.	9	AD 322–400
Ether	The record of the Jared-ites, abridged by Moroni. Their migration from the tower of Babel to America. Their history of political intrigues and wars. Cycles of righteousness and rebellion, leading to final destruction.	15	3100?–580 BC
Moroni	Moroni's final thoughts conclude the Book of Mormon, including an appeal to receive the testimony of the book.	10	AD 400–421

Two other groups mentioned in the Book of Mormon were not descended from Lehi's original party. Mulek and his band fled Jerusalem around the same time as Lehi's family. Little is said about their history. They were discovered by a group of Nephite exiles, who taught them their language and religion. The Nephite leader became their king and the Mulekites were absorbed into the Nephite nation.

The Jaredite nation began at the time of the tower of Babel. When God confused the languages of the people (see Genesis 11), he allowed Jared's family and friends to keep the same dialect. He also promised them a home in a choice new land. The Jaredite band multiplied and prospered in the new world. The book of Ether tells how they built a thriving civilization with a population of millions. Yet their history was marred by civil war and apostasy. Prophets were sent to call the Jaredites to repentance. More often than not, these prophets were reviled, leading to God's judgment. In the end, the Jaredites destroyed themselves in a massive final war. Millions were slain, until only the two opposing kings were left. Coriantumr killed Shiz and survived long enough to see the Mulekites enter the land.

War after War

The Book of Mormon's plot is dominated by accounts of migration and warfare. People groups moved from one location to another, often to escape political oppression or war. Most often, the Nephites battled the Lamanites. Yet a number of wars pitted disaffected Nephite factions against their fellow Nephites, usually over control of the government and often in league with the Lamanites.

The stories of these wars are peppered with great acts of heroism. At one point, a group of converted Lamanites took an oath of nonviolence. Many were slaughtered by other Lamanites before they joined the Nephites for protection. A generation later, their children, who had been too young to take the oath, rallied to arms to defend the Nephites in their time of need. These "two thousand stripling soldiers" (Alma 53:22), led by Helaman, turned the tide of battle through their bravery. Throughout the war, not one of them died in battle.

About 50 BC a new faction entered the story: a band of subversives known as the Gadianton robbers. Originally a criminal cartel founded on the basis of secret knowledge and oaths, the group became a political force. At one time they controlled the Nephite government. At other times, their leaders ruled as warlords on the fringes of society, battling against Nephites and Lamanites alike.

BOOK OF MORMON TIME LINE

Date	Book of Mormon Event	Biblical and Historical Events
3100 BC?	Migration of Jaredites to America	Tower of Babel
600 BC	Migration of Lehi and family to America	
587 BC	Mulekites leave Jerusalem for America	Fall of Jerusalem to the Babylonian Empire
580 BC	Destruction of the Jaredites	
323 BC		Death of Alexander the Great
221 BC		The Great Wall of China completed
180 BC?	Discovery of Mulekites by Nephites	
90 BC	Conversion of Lamanite King Lamoni	
64 BC	Helaman's 2,000 stripling warriors	
63 BC		Jerusalem conquered by Rome
50 BC	Rise of Gadianton robbers	

44 BC		Death of Julius Caesar
AD 34	Appearance of Jesus Christ in America	
AD 35–200	Golden age of righteousness and peace	
AD 70		Destruction of the Jewish temple in Jerusalem
AD 200		Christians persecuted under Roman Emperor Severus
AD 306		Constantine becomes Roman Emperor
AD 385	Nephites exterminated	
AD 401		Augustine's *Confessions* completed
AD 421	Book of Mormon record ends	
AD 447		Attila the Hun comes to power

Cycles of Repentance

While wars are prominent, the Book of Mormon presents itself mainly as a spiritual history. Its overall perspective is that anyone who possessed the Promised Land did so in a covenant relationship with God. If the people were righteous, they would be blessed in the land. If they lived in iniquity, they would be cursed. Then, if they did not repent, they would ultimately be destroyed — as were the Jaredites.

This prospect of blessing and disciplinary cursing in the Book of Mormon creates a spiritual cycle. When the people obeyed God, they prospered. Over time, their material blessing made them proud, and they forgot God. As a result, corruption and immorality increased. In response, God humbled the people through famine or plague, defeat by their enemies, or the breakdown of their society. In distress, the people humbled themselves and repented. As they began to live righteously, God blessed them, and the cycle started anew.

For example, the book of Helaman describes how the Nephites were soundly defeated in battle because their wealth had made them proud:

> And because of this their great wickedness, and their boastings in their own strength, they were left in their own strength; therefore they did not prosper, but were afflicted and smitten, and driven before the Lamanites, until they had lost possession of almost all their lands. (Helaman 4:13)

However, as they began to follow God again, it took only seven years after their crushing defeat for the Nephites to become "exceedingly rich" once more (Helaman 6:9–14).

In keeping with this spiritual theme, many chapters in the Book of Mormon record sermons or extended teachings delivered to the Nephites by their prophets and kings. The narrative also includes several examples of personal spiritual renewal and conversion.

Jesus in the Americas?

The high point of the Book of Mormon story is the appearance of Jesus to the ancient Americans in AD 34. As described in 3 Nephi, Jesus' arrival in America was ushered in by terrible devastation. In a series of natural calamities, many entire cities and their populations were annihilated. Only "the more righteous part of the people were saved" from obliteration (3 Nephi 10:12). After three days of complete darkness, the voice of Jesus spoke, pronouncing judgment on those cities and inviting survivors to come to him for eternal life.

Jesus then descended out of heaven and gave a message much like the Sermon on the Mount. Later he appeared again to a larger multitude. He blessed the people as they worshiped him, healed the sick and lame, and taught them on various subjects before rising back into heaven.

At that time, Jesus commissioned twelve men to lead his church. Three of them received a distinct blessing. They would remain alive until the day of final judgment, traveling incognito among the peoples of the world to serve and perform miracles. Stories of the three Nephites occupy a special place in Mormon folklore even today.

The twelve traveled about teaching, baptizing, and doing miracles. Within three years, the entire population of the land was converted, including Nephites and Lamanites. As a result, a golden age of perfect harmony and peace dawned. Social, political, racial, and economic divisions were erased. Crime ceased. This utopian society lasted for almost two hundred years.

How It All Ended

As before, however, prosperity led to pride. Eventually the perfect society unraveled. Around AD 200, rebellion and wickedness began to take root. False churches arose. Nephites and Lamanites divided from each other. As old evils returned, the wicked eventually vastly outnumbered the righteous. The Gadianton conspiracy was revived and spread widely.

As the people became increasingly corrupt, massive wars erupted between Nephites and Lamanites. The carnage continued for fifty years, until just before AD 400, when the Nephites were exterminated. The Book of Mormon reports over two hundred thousand casualties in one great battle. The Lamanites who survived these wars became ancestors of the American Indians.

© Lir Liu. Image from BigStockPhoto.com

Moroni adorns the LDS temple in Salt Lake City.

During these final years, the prophet Mormon condensed the contents of the vast Nephite records onto one smaller set of gold plates, which he entrusted to his son Moroni. The epic story of these two civilizations ends around AD 421, when Moroni hid the plates in a hill called Cumorah, to be preserved for the instruction of a generation to come.

Joseph Smith claimed that this same Moroni appeared to him as a resurrected being in 1823 to prepare him to receive the ancient Nephite record. The story of how Smith obtained and translated the gold plates of Mormon is one of the most foundational—and controversial—claims of the LDS Church. What do we make of this highly contested story of angels and ancient gold writings? We will explore this intriguing story in the next chapter.

3

THE MYSTERIOUS ORIGIN OF
THE BOOK OF MORMON

> ## Where Did the Book of Mormon Come From?

Every year, thousands of faithful Latter-day Saints relive their heritage by traveling to the historic sites of Mormonism in the eastern United States. A thriving industry offers guided tours to the places where Joseph Smith received his visions, translated the gold plates, and organized the LDS Church. Many tour patrons expect to receive not only an informative excursion but also a deeply emotional and spiritual experience. One vendor enlists participants to perform inspirational readings, dramatic reenactments, and beloved hymns of the faith.

For Mormons, these places are holy. Their history is sacred, a record of supernatural wonders, fulfilled prophecies, and events of global significance. The story of Joseph Smith and the gold plates truly is remarkable. If it is true, the Mormon message deserves to be heeded. But even in the earliest years of Mormonism, many observers contested the authenticity of Smith's experiences. Today, new historical inquiries have raised further doubts about the miraculous story of how the Book of Mormon came to be.

A Mirror of the Times

Born in 1805, Joseph Smith moved with his family to Palmyra, New York, in 1816.[1] His mother, Lucy, was a religious seeker who read the Bible and desired to serve God, but like many of her contemporaries, she failed to find satisfaction in any of the Christian denominations. Joseph Smith Sr. also had a spiritual bent, but he showed little interest in institutional religion. Through a series of dreams, he became convinced that salvation was possible but that the religious world around him lacked the truth.

Like many people of their time, the Smiths were heavily involved in folk magic. Family members practiced various forms of divination, including glass-looking. This involved using a small "peep stone" or "seer stone" to view hidden or invisible objects, such as lost items or buried treasure. In upstate New York, magic practices were common, even among active churchgoers.[2] Joseph Jr. inherited his parents' supernatural worldview along with their religious uncertainty. As a teen, put off by the competitive strife he observed between denominations, he was perplexed about how to be saved and which church was correct.

The First Vision

Smith's career as a prophet began, according to LDS accounts, with a revelation known as the First Vision. At age fourteen, after studying the Bible and visiting local congregations, he decided to ask God directly which church to join. As he prayed, a bright pillar of light descended over his head and two glorious personages appeared above him in the air. One pointed to the other and said, "This is My Beloved Son. Hear Him!" Smith asked these beings which of the churches was right. He was warned to join none of them, for God the Father told him "that all their creeds were an abomination in his sight; that those professors were all corrupt."[3]

By presenting all Christian churches as false, the First Vision story sets the stage for Smith's career as God's instrument to restore original Christianity and for the church he founded to be the only true church. But several different versions of the First Vision predate the official account. These variant accounts differ in many details. In one, Smith says that he determined by reading the Bible that the churches had fallen

© Institute for Religious Research

Joseph Smith's First Vision

away. Yet the official version states that before the vision, he had no idea any of them were wrong. In one account, only Jesus appeared. In another, Smith mentions two unnamed personages, one of whom testifies that Jesus is the Son of God. In yet another version, he speaks of seeing angels but not divine beings. In one account, the vision happened when Smith was sixteen years old. Later versions say that he was fourteen.[4]

Not all Latter-day Saints are familiar with these variant versions of the First Vision. Those who are familiar with them argue that these differences are not contradictions, but merely variations in emphasis. They claim that different occasions called for Smith to recall different aspects of this rich, dynamic experience. A related view is that as Smith's confidence in and understanding of his prophetic calling grew, he gave more of the details than he had before.[5] But for those who do not already have an allegiance to Joseph Smith, the differences raise honest questions as to whether he actually had this vision or merely made it up — and embellished it along the way — to support his claims.

The Gold Plates Emerge

Joseph Smith's second visionary experience introduced him to the Book of Mormon. According to the official story, Smith was seventeen years old when a heavenly messenger appeared in his room one night. The angel identified himself as Moroni, the same person who had buried the ancient Nephite records. He explained that God had a work for Joseph to do.

> He said there was a book deposited, written upon gold plates, giving an account of the former inhabitants of this continent, and the source from whence they sprang. He also said that the fullness of the everlasting Gospel was contained in it, as delivered by the Savior to the ancient inhabitants.[6]

The angel then revealed where the plates were hidden: under a stone on a nearby hill. To ensure he understood the message, Moroni appeared to him three times that same night and again the next day. As instructed, Smith went to the Hill Cumorah and unearthed the gold plates. He was told to return each year on that same date for further instructions. On September 22, 1827, the angel allowed Joseph, now twenty-one, to take possession of the plates, along with two items buried beside them: a breastplate and the Urim and Thummim. The latter was a pair of crystals set in a metal frame like eyeglasses, provided by God as an instrument of translation. Smith was told to protect the plates carefully. He was not to show them to anyone or he would be destroyed.

"By the Gift and Power of God"

The work of translation began in the spring of 1828, with Martin Harris, a Palmyra farmer, acting as scribe. Joseph Smith did not translate the Book of Mormon in a strict sense. He did not study the plates directly. At times, the plates were not even in the same room. Rather,

© Institute for Religious Research

Joseph Smith receives the gold plates from the angel Moroni.

he looked into the Urim and Thummim, where he saw the text of the translation appear. He then dictated several words at a time to his scribe. If correctly written, that phrase would disappear and the next would take its place. Later, instead of the Urim and Thummim, Smith translated using the same magic seer stone with which he had once hunted for buried treasure. He placed the stone in the crown of his hat and held the hat up to his face to exclude the light. The words of the translation appeared in the stone.[7]

After transcribing 116 pages of text, Harris begged Smith for permission to take the manuscript home to show his wife. Reluctantly Joseph agreed. To his horror, the manuscript disappeared. Smith realized that if he tried to reproduce the lost pages, his work as a translator could be tested. He solved the problem by explaining that the gold plates contained two different accounts covering the same time period. He said that God now commanded him to translate the second record instead of reproducing the first—to prevent his enemies from altering the original manuscript as evidence against him. Smith did not resume his dictation until some nine months later, in April 1829, when Oliver Cowdery took over as scribe. From that time, the transcription proceeded rapidly and was completed by June—a pace of over seven printed pages per day. The Book of Mormon was published in the spring of 1830.

For Latter-day Saints, the method and pace of dictation is strong evidence that Joseph Smith could not have composed the Book of Mormon himself. The story is intricate, with intersecting plot lines and hundreds of different character and place names. Yet it displays unity of purpose and themes. It includes detailed descriptions of events, eloquent speeches, and a variety of different voices and perspectives. Using no written notes, with no trial runs or rough drafts, Smith, an uneducated farm boy, dictated the story page after page, without stumbling into contradictions or errors. This could only have been done, Mormons believe, by the power of God.[8]

Traditional Christians have no problem, in principle, with the appearance of an angel to a prophet or with the revelation of divine scripture. But questions arise about Joseph Smith's particular claims. For example, during the years that Smith was preparing to receive the gold plates, he continued to engage in divination. In fact, he was hired by Josiah Stowell to use his seer stone to find a hidden treasure on Stowell's land. In 1826, Smith was brought to court for being a disorderly person and an imposter, based on this treasure-seeking activity.[9]

Non-Mormons are perplexed by the way Smith's glass-looking seems to flow seamlessly into his activity as a prophet. In later years, Smith openly acknowledged his many youthful follies during this period of time. Presumably he was thinking, in part, about his treasure-hunting activities.[10] But how did a magical implement used for occult purposes suddenly become a tool of divine revelation? One LDS scholar suggests that Smith's miraculous gift "evolved naturally out of earlier treasure hunting."[11]

Given God's displeasure with occult activities (Deuteronomy 18:10–14; Ezekiel 13:17–23), this is a difficult evolution to grasp. And if this transition from glass-looker to prophet is credible, I wonder why, in my years growing up as a Mormon, I heard Smith's involvement in magic practices denied by LDS leaders as a slander invented by his enemies.

Some scholars believe that Smith's early experiences with folk magic were recast in more biblical-sounding categories in later years. From time to time, hints of fanciful magic tales surrounding Smith crop up apart from official accounts. For example, later LDS leaders recounted stories told to them by Smith and his cohorts about a cache of artifacts buried in the Hill Cumorah. Oliver Cowdery and Joseph's brother Hyrum both related how they accompanied Joseph into a cave in the hill that was filled with scores of ancient records, weapons, and other relics.[12] These accounts raise questions about the objective reality of Smith's other experiences. Did they really happen? Did Smith only believe that they happened? Or did he make them up?

The Testimony of Witnesses

Shortly after the Book of Mormon transcription was complete and before the gold plates were returned to the angel Moroni, Smith allowed some of his followers to see them. Known as the "three witnesses," Oliver Cowdery, David Whitmer, and Martin Harris signed a statement attesting that an angel showed them the plates and the engravings upon them. Another statement, signed by eight other witnesses, claims that these men "had seen and hefted" the actual gold plates.[13]

Since the plates are no longer available for examination, Latter-day Saints place a great deal of weight on the word of these men—especially the three. Their eyewitness testimony may be the strongest evidence that the gold plates ever existed. Cowdery, Harris, and Whitmer all became disaffected with Joseph Smith and Mormonism at one time or another. But none of them ever recanted their testimony of the gold plates.

To the outside observer, however, some questions arise about this evidence. The three witnesses were not known to be liars. But just what was the nature of their experience? Their statement says that the plates were shown to them "by the power of God, and not of man." In later years, Martin Harris claimed that he saw the plates through "the eyes of faith." Harris had a reputation for visionary experiences and a vivid imagination. David Whitmer referred to his experience as a vision. Thus it is probable that the three witnesses never saw real gold plates with their physical eyes. The visionary nature of their experience makes their testimony less convincing. It is not the kind of evidence, for instance, that would be admitted in a court of law.

Unlike the three, the eight witnesses never claimed to see the plates "by the power of God." Moreover, they said they actually touched the plates. At face value, then, their testimony seems to be rooted in an objective, physical experience. Yet one of the witnesses, Hiram Page, possessed a peep-stone and claimed to receive revelations through it. Another witness, John Whitmer, said that he saw the plates by a supernatural power. Martin Harris claimed that none of the eight witnesses actually saw or handled the gold plates except in a vision.[14]

Another factor diminishes the testimony of these witnesses. In the same generation others were offering similar evidence. A religious sect called the Shakers presented eight witnesses who claimed to see an angel holding their book of scripture. Seven witnesses testified that they had seen and handled another set of ancient plates that God had delivered to James Strang. If we believe the LDS witnesses, we must consider the claims of these others as well. Thus, while the testimony of honest men must carry some weight, those who are not already inclined to believe the story might not find this evidence as strong as it seems.[15]

Could Joseph Smith Have Written the Book of Mormon?

From the earliest days of its publication, people have looked for a connection between the Book of Mormon and literary sources that might have been available to Joseph Smith. For example, Ethan Smith's *A View of the Hebrews* (1823) presents several parallels to the Book of Mormon. Among them is the view, commonly held in America in the early 1800s, that the American Indians were descended from Israelites. But while *A View of the Hebrews* could certainly have informed Smith's imagination, it does not provide a plot or characters.

Some have argued that the Book of Mormon story was plagiarized from an unpublished novel by Solomon Spaulding. This theory depends on demonstrating a connection between Smith and Spaulding, which I do not find convincing. But whether it draws from other sources or not, the Book of Mormon clearly reflects the cultural influences and popular issues of Smith's times.[16]

With or without help from other sources, could Joseph Smith have composed the Book of Mormon? Smith was educated at a level common to his times. But intelligence and imagination are not dependent on education. He was raised in a family receptive to visions and dreams. His mother reports that he would entertain the family with stories about the ancient inhabitants of the Americas, including their dress, cities, warfare, and religion.[17]

Smith started talking about the gold plates over five years before the Book of Mormon was published. During that time, he could have imagined the story in much of its detail. The process of dictation that we may find difficult today was probably easier in a culture adept at oral communication, where storytelling was a common skill. In fact, as I read the Book of Mormon, I see marks of an oral style. Sentences are long and rambling and filled with repetition—as one might expect if the author was speaking extemporaneously.

Joseph Smith dictates the Book of Mormon to a scribe.

From *An Insider's View of Mormon Origins* by Grant Palmer. Used by permission.

I cannot prove absolutely that Joseph Smith did not receive the gold plates from an angel or translate them by the power of God. But the claims made in his story are so remarkable that the burden of proof lies with those who defend it. We are faced with changing versions of the First Vision, fanciful tales of treasure buried in a hill, the transformation of a magic peep stone into a divine instrument of translation, suggestions by witnesses that they saw the gold plates only in a vision, the possibility of literary dependence on other sources, and the innate imagination and ability of Joseph Smith. So it is understandable if non-Mormons have reservations.

Many faithful Latter-day Saints are not aware of these questions. Those who are find the explanations given by Mormon scholars convincing. But for Latter-day Saints, the ultimate proof of the Book of

Mormon comes in the form of a self-validating spiritual experience.[18] Yet Joseph Smith's message is concrete and matter-of-fact. He claimed to possess actual gold plates and located their story in history and on a particular continent. Unfortunately no concrete evidence is available for examination. Without empirical verification, all we can do is compare the plausibility of different theories. Those who are not already committed to the truth of the Book of Mormon or the divine calling of Joseph Smith will find enough questions to cause reasonable doubt.

If we have questions about the origin of the Book of Mormon, what about its contents? What does the Book of Mormon teach, and how does this compare to the Bible? Can Christians embrace its doctrines? The next chapter takes another look inside the Book of Mormon—this time not to understand its story line, but to learn more about its message.

CHAPTER

4

THE FULLNESS OF THE EVERLASTING GOSPEL?

What Does the Book of Mormon Teach?

Most of my family members are faithful Latter-day Saints. As I asked them about their views of the Book of Mormon, one brother-in-law pointed out that the book's title fails to capture its essential message. He sees it mainly as a book about Jesus Christ, with a message that Jesus is the Son of God who died to redeem us from our sins. Supposedly the work of ancient prophets, the Book of Mormon does present a view of Jesus, God, human nature, salvation, and many other important topics. In fact, Joseph Smith wrote that the gold plates contained "the fullness of the everlasting gospel."[1] Yet many central doctrines espoused by the LDS Church are not found in the Book of Mormon. In many ways, its teachings resemble biblical doctrines more than they do the later teachings of Joseph Smith and contemporary Mormonism.

"We Talk of Christ, We Rejoice in Christ ..."

Many Christians are surprised to learn that the Book of Mormon is filled with references to Jesus. For example, six hundred years before Christ, Nephi had a vision of the virgin birth, John the Baptist, Jesus' baptism, his miracles, the calling of the twelve disciples, and Jesus' death on the cross for the sins of the world (1 Nephi 11:13–33). Many other Book of Mormon passages also foretell in detail the life and ministry of Jesus. In fact, references to Jesus appear, on average, about every two verses. Thus Latter-day Saints take to heart 2 Nephi 25:26: "And we talk of Christ, we rejoice in Christ, we preach of Christ, we prophesy of Christ."

The picture of Jesus presented in the Book of Mormon is similar to that of the Bible. Jesus is called Alpha and Omega, the Beloved Son, Redeemer, King, and many other familiar titles. In fact, the Book of Mormon teaches that Jesus is fully God:

> ... the Lord Omnipotent who reigneth, who was, and is from all eternity to all eternity, shall come down from heaven among the children of men.... And he shall be called Jesus Christ, the Son of God, the Father of heaven and earth, the Creator of all things from the beginning. (Mosiah 3:5, 8)

This statue of Jesus occupies center stage at the LDS Temple Square Visitor's Center in Salt Lake City.

The Jesus of the Book of Mormon is the Savior, who "cometh into the world that he may save all men if they will hearken unto his voice"

(2 Nephi 9:21). His suffering on the cross is spoken of frequently, as in Alma 22:14: "And since man had fallen he could not merit anything of himself; but the sufferings and death of Christ atone for their sins." The apex of the Book of Mormon's story is the ministry of the resurrected Jesus on the American continent.

Yet perhaps the Book of Mormon tells us too much about Jesus. It strikes me as odd that the Nephites understood a full-blown New Testament type of gospel, hundreds of years in advance, compared to the patchwork picture revealed to the Old Testament prophets. For instance, when Lehi left Jerusalem, he knew that Jesus would be baptized by John and even foretold specific words that John would say. He understood that the Savior would die and rise from the dead (1 Nephi 10:4–11).

Certainly God could have revealed all this in advance if he chose. But it doesn't seem consistent that he would disclose so much detail to the Nephites but not to the biblical prophets. By contrast to the Book of Mormon, the Old Testament picture of Jesus is so enigmatic that what the Jews expected was quite different from what Jesus actually was when he came. What's more, the only details about Jesus' earthly life found in the Book of Mormon are those also contained in the Bible. One plausible explanation is that Joseph Smith simply wove details about Jesus into the Book of Mormon — details that he knew after the fact — and presented this information as prophecy.

Father, Son, and Holy Ghost

In the Book of Mormon, God the Father is presented as Creator and Supreme Being, worthy to receive prayer and worship. He is a God of wisdom, justice, and mercy.[2] The Holy Ghost, also known as the Spirit of the Lord, empowers prophecy, spiritual enlightenment, and miracles. His presence is given as a gift to those who repent and are converted.[3]

Mormonism denies the traditional doctrine of the Trinity. The Bible teaches that there is only one God, who exists eternally in three persons: Father, Son, and Holy Spirit. By contrast, Mormonism presents a Godhead of three separate beings—three gods—who are united in purpose but not in their essential being.[4] Yet this view does not seem to reflect the Book of Mormon, which speaks "of the Father, and of the Son, and of the Holy Ghost, which is one God, without end. Amen" (2 Nephi 31:21). Another passage teaches that the wicked shall be "arraigned before the bar of Christ the Son, and God the Father, and the Holy Spirit, which is one Eternal God" (Alma 11:44). Elsewhere Jesus is identified as "the very Eternal Father of heaven and earth" (Alma 11:39). These verses certainly sound Trinitarian.

Latter-day Saint teachers explain that the Son is the Father in three ways. He is the Father of creation because he made it. He is the Father of all who accept his atoning sacrifice. He is the Father by divine delegation of authority, so that he is fully authorized and commissioned to speak and act for the Father.[5] In other words, Jesus is sometimes called by the title "Father," but God the Father is a distinct being. Yet the Book of Mormon seems to equate the Father and the Son as one God.

In several other key areas, the Book of Mormon's teaching about God differs markedly from the later teachings of Joseph Smith. For example, Smith declared that God is an exalted man, who was once mortal like us before he became God.[6] Mormonism teaches that God is married and Jesus is literally his spirit child.[7] These concepts are not found anywhere in the Book of Mormon.

A Fall Upward?

The Bible teaches that human beings were created good, but they disobeyed God and thus fell into a darkened moral condition marked by sin. Likewise, the Book of Mormon says that the fall "brought upon all mankind a spiritual death as well as a temporal, that is, they were cut off from the presence of the Lord" and that men and women thus became "carnal, sensual, and devilish, by nature" (Alma 42:9–10). Thus the fall results in a depraved spiritual condition: "For the natural man is an enemy to God, and has been from the fall of Adam" (Mosiah 3:19).

Yet the Book of Mormon introduces a notion that is completely foreign to the Bible when it teaches that Adam's fall was necessary for the advancement of the human race. In 2 Nephi 2:22–23, we learn that it was not good for Adam and Eve to remain in the garden of Eden: "They would have had no children; wherefore they would have remained in a state of innocence, having no joy, for they knew no misery; doing no good, for they knew no sin." Verse 25 concludes that "Adam fell that men might be." In other words, the human race would not exist unless Adam had first sinned. In their Edenic innocence, Adam and Eve could not procreate—even though God had commanded them to multiply and fill the earth. In other words, this view of the fall pits two commandments of God against each other. Adam and Eve could not fulfill the mandate to multiply unless they disobeyed God's directive not to eat from the tree of knowledge.

Again, later teachings of Mormonism go far beyond what the Book of Mormon teaches about the human condition. The LDS Church teaches that we existed in a premortal state as spirit children of God before we were born into this world.[8] It also holds that humans are the same kind of being as God—only less advanced—and that, as such, we have the inherent capacity to become gods ourselves.[9] These doctrines, too, are not found in the Book of Mormon.

"By Grace ... After All We Can Do"

Since human beings are viewed as fallen and separated from God, the Book of Mormon also prescribes how people can be saved. Salvation is achieved by the atonement of Christ and is seen as a new birth into eternal life, which involves a change from the old nature:

And it came to pass that after Aaron had expounded these things unto him, the king said: What shall I do that I may have this eternal life of which thou hast spoken? Yea, what shall I do that I may be born of God, having this wicked spirit rooted out of my breast, and receive his Spirit, that I may be filled with joy, that I may not be cast off at the last day? (Alma 22:15)

Moreover, salvation in the Book of Mormon involves a heavenly reward when a person is resurrected to face the final judgment of their works (Alma 11:41). Those who remain faithful to the end have their sins forgiven and "are received into heaven, that thereby they may dwell with God in a state of never-ending happiness" (Mosiah 2:41). Those who have not repented of their sins are "hewn down and cast into the fire" (Helaman 4:18).

According to the Bible, a person is saved by God's grace, through a response of turning from sin and trusting in the person and work of Jesus Christ. This leads to a changed life characterized by good works. In the Book of Mormon, the human response that secures salvation is fourfold: faith, repentance, and baptism, followed by ongoing faithfulness.

> And he commandeth all men that they must repent, and be baptized in his name, having perfect faith in the Holy One of Israel, or they cannot be saved in the kingdom of God. And if they will not repent and believe in his name, and be baptized in his name, and endure to the end, they must be damned. (2 Nephi 9:23–24)

Grace is mentioned in the Book of Mormon. But in the end, salvation is conditional, as 2 Nephi 25:23 states: "For we know that it is by grace that we are saved, after all we can do." In the Bible grace is God's favor, given freely to those who do not deserve it. But in the Book of Mormon, God's saving gift only applies after a person has made their best effort to be worthy. This relationship between grace and effort is seen in Moroni 10:32:

> Yea, come unto Christ, and be perfected in him, and deny yourselves of all ungodliness; and if ye shall deny yourselves of all ungodliness, and love God with all your might, mind and strength, then is his grace sufficient for you, that by his grace ye may be perfect in Christ.

Notice the progression: if you turn from ungodliness, and if you love God completely, then God's grace is sufficient. The Book of

Mormon, then, teaches salvation by a combination of God's grace added to human exertion.

While Mormonism still affirms the necessity of faith, repentance, baptism, and obedience, Joseph Smith's later teachings about salvation introduced a number of innovations. For example, he taught that there are three heavens with different degrees of glory,[10] that in the highest heaven men and women can become exalted as gods,[11] and that eternal marriage is required for this exalted position.[12] Mormonism also teaches a person has a second chance to repent and turn to Christ after death.[13] None of these ideas are derived from the Book of Mormon.

Personal Revelation

The Book of Mormon has much to say on other topics as well. It foretells the future of Israel. It contains moral instruction about the dangers of pride and other vices. It speaks often about social and ethical issues. At the heart of its message is the promise of personal revelation. Many examples in the book encourage its readers that they can inquire of God for direct input about their lives and can expect a concrete answer. The Book of Mormon portrays Nephite leaders seeking and receiving revelation about doctrinal matters. But personal revelation is not limited to matters so sublime. Nephi inquired of the Lord to learn where to hunt. Nephite generals asked for direction about where and how to attack their enemies.[14]

At one point, Nephi desired to understand the meaning of one of his father's visions. He inquired of God, knowing that "he that diligently seeketh shall find; and the mysteries of God shall be unfolded unto them" (1 Nephi 10:19). By contrast, his brothers could not understand the vision. They did not inquire of God because they assumed that "the Lord maketh no such thing known unto us" (1 Nephi 15:9). What separated Nephi from his wicked brothers was his response to the prospect of personal revelation from God.

The principle of direct, individual revelation is established not only by example but also by invitation. Moroni 10:5 says, "By the power of the Holy Ghost ye may know the truth of all things." On that basis, the reader is encouraged to ask God if the Book of Mormon is true, with the promise that God will make its truth known to those who are sincere.

Are Mormons Christians?

We have seen that the Book of Mormon has much in common with biblical doctrine. In particular, it emphasizes Jesus Christ and portrays him as the divine Creator and Redeemer of the world. Mormons revere Jesus. They seek to know, follow, and obey him. This is why Latter-day Saints are confused and often offended when others assert that they are not Christians.

I try to avoid arguing about who is or is not a Christian. I can say with confidence that, because of its teachings about God, humanity, and salvation, the LDS Church stands outside of historic, biblical Christianity. I personally do not believe a person can find eternal life by following the LDS approach to salvation. But I can't look inside other individuals to discern their spiritual condition. Besides, the argument is rarely fruitful, for it revolves around differing assumptions about what defines a valid Christian. As my brother-in-law says, "I have always been profoundly bothered by the idea that the definition of one's 'Christianity' hinges on doctrinal details rather than adherence to the ideals that Christ taught."

Latter-day Saints are not blind to how often people with correct biblical beliefs fail to obey or emulate Jesus. Thus it seems wiser to discuss the substance of our hope in Christ and what it actually means to be right with God rather than to debate about mere labels.

The Fullness of the Gospel

As I mentioned above, the Book of Mormon is said to contain "the fulness of the everlasting gospel." This raises a question, since the Book of Mormon says nothing about a number of essential LDS beliefs about God and eternity. My nephew explained his perspective on this question:

When we say that the book contains the fullness of the gospel, we're not saying it contains every piece of doctrine, but that it contains the tools to obtain the fullness, pointing specifically to Joseph Smith but more generally to the existence of modern-day prophets and the validity of the Restoration.

I would say in response that perhaps when Joseph Smith produced the Book of Mormon, it encompassed what he considered at that time to be the complete gospel. But over time, as he developed new doctrines, his theology became increasingly distant from both the Book of Mormon and the Bible. These later doctrinal innovations are developed in other Mormon books. The Book of Mormon stands as only one volume of Joseph Smith's prophetic writings. In the next chapter, we will examine how the Book of Mormon relates to other LDS holy books.

NEW SCRIPTURES FOR THE LAST DAYS

> ## How Does the Book of Mormon Relate to Other LDS Scriptures?

On the Christmas of my sixteenth year, my parents gave me my first "triple combination" — three books of Mormon scripture bound in one volume. It was a significant gift, showing their commitment to their holy books and their encouragement to me to make these scriptures a central part of my life. I still have it. Printed on over nine hundred thin, parchment-like pages and bound in leather, it contains the Book of Mormon, the Doctrine and Covenants, and the Pearl of Great Price. Together with the King James Version of the Bible, these are considered to be divinely inspired and are called the standard works of the LDS Church. While many Mormons carry the triple combination, others use a "quad" — which includes the King James Version under the same leather cover with the other standard works.

The LDS View of Scripture

Historically, Christians have seen the Bible alone as God's final, authoritative word to humanity. By contrast, Mormons do not view the Bible — or even their other scriptures — as containing all of God's words. Joseph Smith wrote: "We believe all that God has revealed, all that He does now reveal, and we believe that He will yet reveal many great and important things pertaining to the Kingdom of God."[1]

Latter-day Saints believe that many ancient books of scripture will one day be restored. For example, the Doctrine and Covenants refers to the book of Enoch that will be available "in due time" (D&C 107:57). The Book of Mormon foretells that the records of the lost ten tribes of Israel will eventually be added to the scriptures (2 Nephi 29:11–13). It also promises that a fuller account of the words of Jesus to the Nephites will one day be unsealed (3 Nephi 26:6–8).

The LDS Church also claims to have prophets who speak for God today. The inspired words of these prophets, as given through Church conferences and publications, are treated as scripture.[2] Speaking of those ordained to proclaim God's truth, the Doctrine and Covenants 68:4 says:

> And whatsoever they shall speak when moved upon by the Holy Ghost shall be scripture, shall be the will of the Lord, shall be the mind of the Lord, shall be the word of the Lord, shall be the voice of the Lord, and the power of God unto salvation.

Every LDS Church president is viewed by Mormons as a prophet, seer, and revelator. Thus no holy book carries final authority in Mormonism. In the end, the word of a living prophet stands above the authority of written scripture.[3] For instance, a prophet could be inspired with revelation that provides a new or fuller interpretation of some scriptural text. Statements of LDS leaders are formally added to the pages of the standard works from time to time.

By contrast, the historic Christian position is that God's conclusive revelation to humanity has already been given in the person of Jesus Christ (Hebrews 1:1–2), as elaborated in the Bible. But even if we do allow for the possibility of additional scripture, the Bible warns often of false prophets and thus teaches that any message claiming to come from God must be evaluated. Deuteronomy 13:1–3 suggests that the test is whether or not the new revelation conforms to what God has already revealed about himself. Because of these biblical warnings, Christians have always been suspicious of new claims to divine truth.

AP Photo/Douglas C. Pizac

Latter-day Saints consider Church President
Thomas S. Monson to be a latter-day prophet of God.

We are also cautious because history affords many examples of religious leaders who have tried to undermine the Bible's unique authority in order to introduce their own.

The Doctrine and Covenants

In his role as a prophet, Joseph Smith gave numerous revelations that were published in 1835 as the Doctrine and Covenants — a "collection of divine revelations and inspired declarations given for the establishment and regulation of the kingdom of God on the earth in the last days."[4] Of the 138 separate chapters — known as sections — of the Doctrine and Covenants, 135 were given by Joseph Smith. Three of his successors contributed one apiece, and it is possible that more revelations will be added in the future. The book also includes two official declarations, from 1890 and 1978, which give direction for important issues of LDS practice.

Many sections in the Doctrine and Covenants deal with mundane matters of governing the LDS Church in its early years. Some sections are not strictly revelations but contain letters, reports, and statements. A number of sections relate to the development of the Church's structure by defining offices and creating governing bodies. Some sections expand on biblical themes, while others contain prophecies of the future. The Doctrine and Covenants also contains a number of unique teachings central to Mormonism, including eternal marriage, polygamy, salvation for the dead, and the LDS priesthood.[5]

KEY TEACHINGS OF THE DOCTRINE AND COVENANTS	
Section	Contents
76	Those who attain the highest level of heaven are called gods.
84	The basis and function of the greater ("Melchizedek") and lesser ("Aaronic") priesthoods of Mormonism.
88	Heaven has three distinct levels, of differing glory: the celestial kingdom, the telestial kingdom, and the terrestrial kingdom.
89	The "Word of Wisdom" outlines Mormon dietary laws, including prohibition of tobacco and alcohol.

93	Human beings are eternal and uncreated, and the soul is divine in nature.
128	Baptism is performed for the salvation of those who have already died.
131	Eternal marriage is a requirement for exaltation in the highest heaven.
132	Eternal marriage continues the family unit after death and is required to become a god. A man may marry more than one wife.
138	Salvation is possible for those who have died, if people on earth perform required temple ordinances for them.
Official Declaration 1	Called the "Manifesto," this 1890 declaration banned polygamy.
Official Declaration 2	In 1978, the priesthood was granted to worthy men of all races.

The Book of Moses

The Pearl of Great Price contains three shorter works, beginning with the Book of Moses. In 1830, Joseph Smith claimed to receive an inspired expansion of the Bible's book of Genesis. Along with a vision experienced by the biblical prophet Moses, additional material is inserted into the text of Genesis 1–6 to expound on topics like the nature of creation, the role of Satan, the family of Adam and Eve, and the sin of Cain. For example, the Book of Moses expands the story of Enoch, which occupies four verses in the Bible (Genesis 5:21–24), into over a hundred verses.

The Book of Moses introduces several unique ideas not found in the Bible. It teaches that all things were created spiritually first before they were created materially. It describes how God chose Jesus over Satan to become the Savior of the world and how Satan, thus rebuffed, rebelled against God and was cast out of heaven to become the devil. It portrays Adam and the ancients as having a full knowledge of Jesus Christ and the plan of salvation from the very beginning.[6]

The Book of Abraham

Also part of the Pearl of Great Price, the Book of Abraham has a unique origin. A traveling exhibitor sold four mummies and some papyrus scrolls to the Mormons in 1835. Joseph Smith declared that one of the scrolls contained the "writings of Abraham while he was in Egypt,"[7] which Smith proceeded to translate.

The Book of Abraham provides the basis for several unique LDS doctrines. In Abraham's vision of the universe, he learns that the throne of God is found near a star called Kolob. The same vision depicts human spirits, called "intelligences," as being eternal and uncreated. It shows these spirits making decisions in a great council, prior to being born on this earth. An account of creation, similar to Genesis 1–2, portrays multiple gods involved in the formation of the universe.[8]

The story of the Book of Abraham took an interesting twist in 1966. The papyrus scrolls had been lost after Joseph Smith's death until parts of the collection turned up in New York City's Metropolitan Museum of Art. A portion of the scroll that Smith supposedly translated was identified by comparing it to his notes and drawings. Yet when modern scholars analyzed the papyrus, they found it to be a funeral text commonly buried with mummies. The papyrus dated from

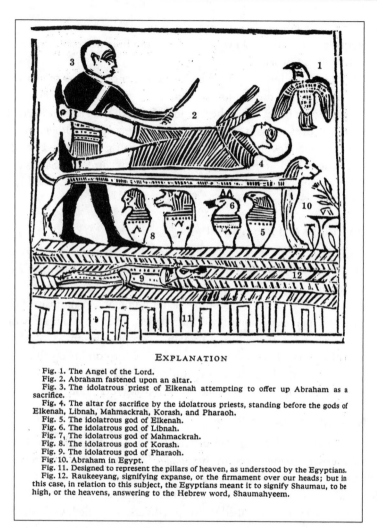

EXPLANATION

Fig. 1. The Angel of the Lord.

Fig. 2. Abraham fastened upon an altar.

Fig. 3. The idolatrous priest of Elkenah attempting to offer up Abraham as a sacrifice.

Fig. 4. The altar for sacrifice by the idolatrous priests, standing before the gods of Elkenah, Libnah, Mahmackrah, Korash, and Pharaoh.

Fig. 5. The idolatrous god of Elkenah.

Fig. 6. The idolatrous god of Libnah.

Fig. 7. The idolatrous god of Mahmackrah.

Fig. 8. The idolatrous god of Korash.

Fig. 9. The idolatrous god of Pharaoh.

Fig. 10. Abraham in Egypt.

Fig. 11. Designed to represent the pillars of heaven, as understood by the Egyptians.

Fig. 12. Raukeeyang, signifying expanse, or the firmament over our heads; but in this case, in relation to this subject, the Egyptians meant it to signify Shaumau, to be high, or the heavens, answering to the Hebrew word, Shaumahyeem.

Joseph Smith copied this figure from an Egyptian papyrus and provided his interpretation of the hieroglyphic characters below.

Originally published in *Times and Seasons*, March 1, 1842.

at least fifteen hundred years after the time of Abraham. In fact, the contents had nothing to do with Abraham and bore no resemblance to Joseph Smith's translation.[9]

LDS scholars have responded with a number of theories to explain why the writing on the scrolls does not match the text of the Book of Abraham. Some believe that the text Joseph Smith translated is located on portions of the scrolls that have not been recovered. Others think that the original Egyptian text acted as a catalyst that prompted Smith to receive a revelation directly from God.[10] Many Latter-day Saints are simply unaware of any problems with the Book of Abraham. The LDS Church has never issued an official explanation.

The Writings of Joseph Smith

The final segment of the Pearl of Great Price includes three works written by Joseph Smith. The first is Smith's revision of Matthew 24, to which he added almost five hundred words. The second, called "Joseph Smith — History," recounts the founding of Mormonism. The third part is an explanation of Mormon beliefs. The thirteen brief Articles of Faith found there do not provide a complete summary of LDS doctrine. Rather, they introduce a few basic Mormon beliefs like the existence of God, the ordinances required for salvation, the need for priesthood authority, and the role of continuing revelation.

A New Version of the Bible

In 1833, Joseph Smith completed a revision of the Bible. Working from the King James Version, he resolved contradictions, corrected what he saw as errors, and added what he claimed were lost portions. All in all, more than three thousand individual verses were changed. The amended version is called the Inspired Version or the Joseph Smith Translation, although it is not a translation in any ordinary sense. Smith had not studied the biblical languages. His changes were not based on any review of ancient sources but on what he claimed was direct revelation from God.

The LDS Church has never published a version of the Joseph Smith Translation. No one can say why, although some of Smith's modifications contradict other LDS scripture. But while the official LDS version of the Bible is the King James Version, Smith's revision is frequently cited in the footnotes and cross-references found in the LDS standard works.[11]

We have learned that Latter-day Saints consider the Bible to be divinely inspired and that many of the doctrines of the Book of Mormon resemble biblical teachings. Yet the elevation of other books as scripture, along with Joseph Smith's efforts to revise the Bible, suggests that the Bible does not have the same role in Mormonism as it does in historic Christianity. In our next chapter, we will take a look at the complex relationship between the Book of Mormon and the Bible.

6

ANOTHER TESTAMENT OF JESUS CHRIST

How Does the Book of Mormon Relate to the Bible?

My brother's son, who is an active Latter-day Saint, once told me how the Book of Mormon functions for him. He told me about a time when some fellow college students—who were mostly agnostic or atheistic—were discussing the reliability of the Bible and its stories. He recounts his response:

> I agreed with them that there were mistranslations and things lost, but I had to draw a line. I remember stating that one reason I believed in God and Jesus Christ as described in the Bible wasn't just because of my testimony of the Bible, but also because of my testimony of the Book of Mormon. For me, the belief in the Book of Mormon prevents me from throwing out the Bible in a very secular world. In some ways, the Book of Mormon allows Mormons to rationalize the strange position of admitting the fallacy of the biblical text as we have it today, but at the same time not denying the relevance of the Bible nor denying the existence of God and the divinity and essential role of Christ.

My nephew's experience captures two basic LDS ideas about the Bible. First, although it is divine scripture, today's Bible is inaccurate and incomplete. Second, the Book of Mormon is a corroborating witness that supports the Bible's message. But a closer look at the relationship between the two books suggests that the Book of Mormon may have borrowed much of its content directly from the Bible.

The introduction to the Book of Mormon calls it "a volume of scripture comparable to the Bible," which "contains, as does the Bible, the fulness of the everlasting gospel." The Book of Mormon's style and language is reminiscent of the Bible's King James Version (KJV). Hundreds of phrases in the Book of Mormon echo familiar biblical wording. Entire chapters of Isaiah are inserted within its text.[1] Much like the Bible, the Book of Mormon is divided into books with chapters and verses, each named after its author. In fact, converts to early Mormonism were convinced, in part, because the Book of Mormon seemed to confirm and to be confirmed by the Bible.[2]

"We Believe the Bible to Be the Word of God ..."

The Book of Mormon both validates and calls into question the status of the Bible.[3] The eighth Article of Faith summarizes the relationship: "We believe the Bible to be the word of God as far as it is translated correctly; we also believe the Book of Mormon to be the word of God."[4]

We have seen that Latter-day Saints accept both the Bible and the Book of Mormon as divine scripture. In the curriculum for LDS high school students, one year each is devoted to the Old Testament, the New Testament, and the Book of Mormon. The same is true in the weekly Sunday school class conducted in every LDS congregation.

The Book of Mormon presents itself as verifying, not replacing the Bible. Every Book of Mormon published since 1981 bears the subtitle: "Another Testament of Jesus Christ." In 3 Nephi 23:1, Jesus commanded the Nephites to study the words of Isaiah. First Nephi 13:39–40, speaking of the Book of Mormon and the Bible, predicts that "these last records, which thou hast seen among the Gentiles, shall establish the truth of the first, which are of the twelve apostles of the Lamb."

"... As Far As It Is Translated Correctly"

Paradoxically, the Book of Mormon also presents the Bible as a deficient document, so mishandled over the years that important truths

have been lost. First Nephi 13:26 foresees a "great and abominable church" that would corrupt the Bible by taking away "from the gospel of the Lamb many parts which are plain and most precious; and also many covenants of the Lord have they taken away."

While the eighth Article of Faith casts doubt on the Bible's translation, the real issue seems to be the Bible's transmission—how the Bible has been copied and handed down. For centuries, the Bible was passed on by scribes who copied the text by hand. Despite their meticulous work, a number of typical copying errors can be identified. The eye might lose its place by skipping to the same word in a different line. A copyist might accidentally add a familiar word or phrase from his memory of a similar-sounding passage.

But the implication of 1 Nephi 13 is that corrupt scribes intentionally changed the Bible's text in order to alter its meaning. Yet no one can demonstrate any specific changes in the Bible of that sort. In fact, by comparing the various manuscripts, the Bible's text can be established as highly trustworthy.[5] In graduate school, I studied the text of Isaiah found in the Dead Sea Scrolls, which predated the oldest previously known copy of Isaiah by one thousand years. Even over ten centuries of copying, the two texts showed only trivial differences. Far from many "plain and precious things" having been removed, no major biblical doctrine is affected by any scribal error.

"A Bible, a Bible; We Have Got a Bible"

The Book of Mormon also challenges those who hold the Bible to be God's complete and final revelation. Second Nephi 29:3 predicts: "Many of the Gentiles shall say: A Bible! A Bible! We have got a Bible, and there cannot be any more Bible." The passage argues that, since the world contains many nations, we can expect God to speak to many different peoples. Verse 10 concludes the case for more scripture beyond the Bible: "Wherefore, because that ye have a Bible ye need not suppose that it contains all my words; neither need ye suppose that I have not caused more to be written."

Thus the Bible is depicted in the Book of Mormon as both corrupted and incomplete.

The Book of Mormon in the Bible

Latter-day Saints believe that several passages in the Bible actually refer to the Book of Mormon. For example, in John 10:16, Jesus told his disciples, "I have other sheep that are not of this sheep pen. I must bring them also. They too will listen to my voice." To Mormons, these "other sheep" are the Book of Mormon peoples. Yet the traditional understanding among a cross-section of Christians is that Jesus was talking about the Gentiles, who would later be gathered with believing Jews into one people of God.

Isaiah 29 is especially significant to Mormons. They interpret verse 4 as prophesying the Book of Mormon coming forth out of the ground: "And thou shalt be brought down, and shalt speak out of the ground, and thy speech shall be low out of the dust, and thy voice shall be, as of one that hath a familiar spirit, out of the ground, and thy speech shall whisper out of the dust" (KJV). Bible scholars understand this as a warning against the arrogance of Jerusalem. Once proud and lofty, the city would be deprived of strength and humbled so low that its voice could only be heard like a feeble whisper from the dust.

Isaiah 29:11–12 is also understood to predict events surrounding the Book of Mormon.

> And the vision of all is become unto you as the words of a book that is sealed, which men deliver to one that is learned, saying, Read this, I pray thee: and he saith, I cannot; for it is sealed: And the book is delivered to him that is not learned, saying, Read this, I pray thee: and he saith, I am not learned. (KJV)

Mormons believe this describes the experience of Martin Harris. Joseph Smith gave Harris a drawing of characters copied from the golden plates, which Harris presented to noted scholar Charles Anthon in New York City. Anthon denied that the characters were authentic. But to Mormons, the point is that while Anthon—the learned man—could not read them, the unlearned Smith could. In context, however, these verses describe God's verdict against the people of Jerusalem. Verse 10 (KJV) says, "The LORD ... hath closed your eyes." The truths revealed by the prophets became inaccessible to the people—sealed from the comprehension of wise and ignorant alike. Contrary to the LDS interpretation, neither the learned nor the unlearned could read the sealed book.

Latter-day Saints also understand Ezekiel 37 as predicting the Book of Mormon. In verses 16–17, God told Ezekiel to write on one stick "For Judah" and on another "For Joseph," and to join the two sticks into one. This would symbolize God's future action in verse 19:

> Behold, I will take the stick of Joseph, which is in the hand of Ephraim, and the tribes of Israel his fellows, and will put them

A drawing of Book of Mormon characters presented to Dr. Charles Anthon by Martin Harris

The original is in the archives of the Community of Christ.

with him, even with the stick of Judah, and make them one stick, and they shall be one in mine hand. (Ezek. 37:19, KJV)

In LDS thinking, the stick of Judah represents the Bible, the scripture of the Jews. The stick of Joseph represents the scripture of the Nephites, who were descended from Joseph. The joining of the two sticks was fulfilled when the Book of Mormon emerged alongside the Bible as God's word. But verses 21–22 explain that the prophecy is about the restoration of God's people into one kingdom again.

Behold, I will take the children of Israel from among the heathen, whither they be gone, and will gather them on every side, and bring them into their own land: And I will make them one nation in the land … neither shall they be divided into two kingdoms any more at all. (KJV)

After Solomon, the kingdom of Israel was divided into two: Israel (sometimes called Ephraim) and Judah. Later, both were taken captive and dispersed by foreign empires. Ezekiel 37 foresees a time when the two nations—like the two sticks representing them—will be joined into one kingdom.

The Bible in the Book of Mormon

As stated, the Book of Mormon contains extensive material in common with the Bible. The first type of shared content consists of simple repetition or direct quotation, including frequent phrases such as "it came to pass" and "verily, verily I say unto you."[6]

A second type of parallel involves interpretative changes to a biblical text. For example, note how 2 Nephi 2:18 expands the biblical account of Eve's temptation. The additional material is itself parallel to Revelation 12:9 and John 8:44.

"And the serpent said unto the woman, Ye shall not surely die: For God doth know that in the day ye eat thereof, then your eyes shall be opened, and ye shall be as gods, knowing good and evil."	Genesis 3:4–5 (KJV)
2 Nephi 2:18	"And because he had fallen from heaven, and had become miserable forever, he sought also the misery of all mankind. Wherefore, he said unto Eve, yea, even that old serpent, who is the devil, who is the father of all lies, wherefore he said: Partake of the forbidden fruit, and ye shall not die, but ye shall be as God, knowing good and evil."

Third, the Book of Mormon contains structural parallels to the Bible. These include literary forms, common motifs, character types, and similar types of events. For instance, the conversion of Alma in Mosiah 27 has many features in common with the story of Paul's conversion in Acts 9.

Alma	Paul
Seeking to the destroy the church	Persecuting the church
Confronted in a vision by an angel	Confronted in a vision by Jesus
Fell to the earth	Fell to the earth
Asked: "Why persecutest thou the church of God?"	Asked: "Why persecutest thou Me?"
Struck dumb	Struck blind
Became an ardent servant of Christ	Became an ardent servant of Christ

All of this shared content raises the question of whether the common material comes from independent sources or whether Joseph Smith in the Book of Mormon simply copied from the Bible. Let's consider these alternatives based on two specific cases.

First, Jesus' address to the Nephites (3 Nephi 12–14) contains much in common with the biblical Sermon on the Mount (Matthew 5–7). Commenting on these similarities, one LDS scholar admits that 3 Nephi is "so blatantly familiar that it almost begs to be labeled (and often has been) facile plagiarism."[7] In fact, the Book of Mormon seems to anticipate the charge of borrowing in 2 Nephi 29:8: "Know ye not that the testimony of two nations is a witness unto you that I am God, that I remember one nation like unto another? Wherefore, I speak the same words unto one nation like unto another." In this case, the similarities between 3 Nephi and Matthew could simply be the result of Jesus having the same message for his disciples in both nations—despite significant differences in the two cultural settings.

Second, the Book of Mormon also contains more than nineteen complete chapters in common with Isaiah. According to the story, Lehi's people carried from Jerusalem a copy of the Old Testament scriptures engraved on plates of brass. As a result, "many quotations from these plates, citing Isaiah and other biblical and nonbiblical prophets, appear in the Book of Mormon."[8] But several lines of evidence raise the question of whether Joseph Smith derived the Isaiah passages directly from the KJV rather than from an ancient source.

Consider just one type of evidence. Biblical scholarship has advanced a great deal since the KJV was translated. The discovery of ancient libraries, in languages closely related to biblical Hebrew, has given us a better understanding of the original text of Isaiah. Thus a number of passages that were obscure to the KJV translators are now more clear. But a close look at the Isaiah passages in the Book of Mormon reveals that some of the misunderstandings found in the KJV also appear in the Book of Mormon. This suggests a direct relationship. Could it be that Joseph Smith simply copied the Isaiah portions from the Bible?

In response, some LDS scholars posit that God allowed Smith to translate into the familiar language of the KJV wherever it agreed substantially with the Nephite version. Others have claimed that the Book of Mormon sometimes reflects better Hebrew manuscripts than those available to the KJV translators. But many scholars find the examples given unconvincing. In any case, these approaches do not explain how errors from the KJV would find their way into the Book of Mormon.[9]

The extensive content shared between the KJV and the Book of Mormon and the nature of the parallels create the strong impression that the Book of Mormon was produced after the King James Version. But Latter-day Saints maintain that the Book of Mormon's ancient provenance can be established in other ways. In chapter 7, we will consider whether the Book of Mormon was produced in the nineteenth century or in the distant past.

7

SEARCH FOR A MISSING CIVILIZATION

Is the Book of Mormon Really an Ancient Book?

As a teenager, I remember the excitement I felt the evening my father and I were invited to visit the ruins of Central America. I envisioned a fascinating adventure to discover the lost cities of the Book of Mormon lands. We never made the trip, although thousands of Latter-day Saints have. Many more have imagined the journey through the various picture books available that compare Book of Mormon stories to ancient American sites.

To Latter-day Saints, the Book of Mormon is an ancient record of great cities, peoples at war, and the rise and fall of nations. They look for its mark on the landscape of America. But archaeology has failed to unearth any concrete evidence for the Book of Mormon. In response, LDS scholars seek to validate the book's antiquity by seeking similarities to the ancient Near East. Others see stronger connections between the Book of Mormon and Joseph Smith's own times.

The Silent Testimony of Archaeology

From the beginning, Latter-day Saints have made various attempts to reconstruct Book of Mormon geography on the American map. The most common approach today locates the story largely in Central America and Mexico, the region known as Mesoamerica. LDS authors have published elaborate suggestions, complete with full color photographs, about how ancient Mesoamerican cultures might parallel the

Book of Mormon peoples.[1] But LDS writers admit that all of this is pure conjecture. One Brigham Young University professor puts it like this: "No one has found any inscriptional evidence for, or material remains that can be tied directly to any of the persons, places or things mentioned in the book."[2]

© Steve Estvanik. Image from BigStockPhoto.com

Latter-day Saints interpret the ancient ruins of Central America as Book of Mormon artifacts.

Consider some examples. The Book of Mormon peoples are described using gold, silver, iron, brass, and copper. The mining, smelting, and casting of metal ores require special tools and complex processes that leave traces in the archaeological record. But scholars generally agree that metallurgy was not introduced into Mesoamerica until several centuries after the Book of Mormon story ends. What's more, the Book of Mormon mentions the use of steel swords. But metal swords were not known in Mesoamerica before the Spanish conquest.[3]

The Book of Mormon also speaks of many different kinds of animals, mostly those familiar in the Old World, like cattle, sheep, goats, and horses. But none of these have been found in any archaeological setting that dates to Book of Mormon times. Unlike the deer, jaguar, peccary, tapir, and other native species, the horse has never been found depicted in any of thousands of samples of Mesoamerican art — in spite of its impressive appearance.[4]

The Book of Mormon contains anachronisms — that is, events or objects that appear out of the proper time period in which one would expect them to be present. To give just one example, Alma 16:13 describes how Nephite evangelists "went forth preaching repentance to the people ... in their synagogues, which were built after the manner of the Jews." The Book of Mormon mentions synagogues twenty-five times. But synagogues were not developed by the Jews until four hundred years after Lehi left Jerusalem. How could the writer have known how the Jews built their synagogues?

To Latter-day Saints, raising issues like this will probably seem like an "anti-Mormon" attack. A sincere inquirer should not be expected to ignore honest questions that bear on the Book of Mormon's credibility. Yet we should raise these questions with sensitivity and humility.

New World archaeology is still a young science. Perhaps some day, an artifact or inscription will be unearthed to validate the Book of Mormon. By contrast, archaeology has repeatedly demonstrated the Bible's historical and geographical reliability. The use of metals, as described in the Bible, has been verified at a number of sites in the Near East. A traveler today can visit the site of ancient Capernaum, where Jesus lived, or Ephesus, where the apostle Paul traveled.[5]

A few years ago I visited the British Museum in London. There I saw a series of massive stone panels from ancient Nineveh, carved during the reign of Assyria's King Sennacherib to commemorate the defeat of the Israelite city Lachish. Lachish is mentioned in the Bible, as is Sennacherib's military campaign in Israel. But even after decades of archaeological work in the New World, it seems to me that the best

Mormon apologists can do is create an aura of plausibility by suggesting vague similarities between the Book of Mormon and ancient Mesoamerica.

Denied by DNA

Recent advances in DNA research have challenged the traditional LDS understanding of where the American Indians came from, leading some to question the credibility of the Book of Mormon's basic story. The predominant hypothesis of mainstream science is that all Native Americans are of Asian origin. This view is supported by extensive DNA sampling of American Indian populations.

The traditional LDS view, still held by most Mormons, is that, as children of Lehi, Native Americans are of Semitic origin. Latter-day Saints have believed this because it was taught by Joseph Smith and is the most straightforward way to read the Book of Mormon text. But widespread testing of Native American DNA affords no evidence of any relationship with Semitic peoples.

While some LDS scholars claim that DNA results are inconclusive and thus do not undermine the traditional view, others have adopted the hypothesis that most Native Americans are of Asian origin, while a small subset is Semitic. If so, Nephites and Lamanites made up only a small portion of the total New World population during the Book of Mormon's time frame.[6]

The LDS Church has seemingly acknowledged that the DNA evidence carries some weight. For example, the introduction to the 1981 edition of the Book of Mormon identifies the Lamanites as "the principal ancestors of the American Indians." The 2006 edition states that the Lamanites "are among the ancestors of the American Indians."[7] This change accommodates the current scientific consensus at the expense of the traditional LDS view. But if the Nephite and Lamanite clans were not alone in the Americas, it seems odd that the Book of Mormon never mentions the numerous people who must have lived in surrounding lands and who surely would have interacted with them.

Are the people of Central America descended from the Lamanites?

Internal versus External Evidence

Lacking external, physical evidence, LDS scholars have turned from spade to book, hoping to establish an ancient provenance for the Book of Mormon by linking it to ancient Near Eastern texts and practices. The idea is that if the Book of Mormon accurately reflects Near Eastern elements that Joseph Smith could not have known and that cannot be traced to the Bible, then it must be taken seriously as an ancient text, even without archaeological proofs.[8] Yet this approach can be highly speculative. The pioneer of this method, Hugh Nibley, explains it like this:

> While Book of Mormon students readily admit that no direct, concrete evidence currently exists substantiating the links with the ancient Near East that are noted in the book, evidence can be adduced—largely external and circumstantial—that commands respect for the claims of the Book of Mormon concerning its ancient Near Eastern background.[9]

For the typical Latter-day Saint, circumstantial evidence is enough. Even though many of the parallels break down upon close inspection, those who are already committed to the Book of Mormon will find them convincing. Their testimony of the Book of Mormon is based on a spiritual experience, not on external verification. Thus LDS scholars merely need to provide enough of an argument to reassure believers and to hold the critics at bay.

Literary Evidence

The first type of internal evidence for the Book of Mormon has to do with its language and style. If the Book of Mormon peoples came from Jerusalem, the root language behind the book would be Hebrew. Thus LDS scholars believe that the presence of Hebrew literary and grammatical patterns, called Hebraisms, give evidence of its ancient origin. The most fundamental problem with this approach is that the Book of Mormon is only available to us in translated form. Without an original document to compare, we simply cannot know whether the Hebraisms we observe are rooted in some Hebrew original or result from factors in the English text.

One example of a Hebraism in the Book of Mormon is chiasm.[10] Chiasm occurs when a series of terms are stated and then repeated in reverse order, forming a mirror-like reflection. The elements of a chiasm follow the pattern A^1-B^1-B^2-A^2, as in Isaiah 6:10 (KJV):

A^1: Make the *heart* of this people fat,

    B^1: and make their *ears* heavy,

        C^1: and shut their *eyes*;

        C^2: lest they see with their *eyes*,

    B^2: and hear with their *ears*,

A^2: and understand with their *heart*, and convert, and be healed.

No one disputes that chiasm appears in the Book of Mormon (see Alma 41:13–14). But does this reflect a Hebrew basis of the text? After all, chiasm is not unique to the Hebrew language. Any time a reciprocal relationship or action is described or a series of items is repeated in reverse order, chiasm will result. The common phrase, "A place for everything, and everything in its place," is a chiasm. Thus chiasm can arise by coincidence.

Moreover, Joseph Smith's familiarity with biblical language could account for chiasm occurring in his writings, whether intentionally or not. This explains why chiasm crops up in Smith's writings outside the Book of Mormon. Let me give just one example, from Doctrine and Covenants 3:2.

A^1: For God doth not walk in crooked paths,

    B^1: neither doth he turn to the right hand nor to the left,

    B^2: neither doth he vary from that which he hath said,

A^2: therefore his paths are straight....

A cursory reading of the Doctrine and Covenants reveals other passages that have elements of chiasm, such as Section 6:33–34 and Section 43:2–6. Since these passages are neither ancient nor Hebrew in origin, they diminish the relevance of chiasm in the Book of Mormon.

LDS apologists also claim to find names in the Book of Mormon that are found in ancient Near Eastern sources but not in the Bible.[11] For example, the name Alma has been found in Jewish documents from about AD 132. But without knowing what the original Hebrew spelling of these names might have been, no one can know whether any Book of Mormon name is truly parallel to a Near Eastern name or not. Moreover, many of the names listed by LDS scholars could easily be derived from biblical names with only slight modification: Sam from Samuel, Josh from Joshua, Sariah from Sarah, Chemish from Chemosh, and so forth.[12]

One challenge in trying to establish Hebraic literary parallels is that the Book of Mormon is riddled with the language of the Bible. As illustrated with chiasm, most of the Hebraisms identified in the Book of Mormon can also be found in modern writings of Joseph Smith.[13] This suggests that these language forms do not come from an ancient

Hebrew source, but from Smith consciously or unconsciously imitating the language of the Bible.

Parallels to Ancient Practices

To establish the Book of Mormon as an ancient work, LDS scholars also point to parallels between events and practices described therein to similar practices in the ancient Near East. Thus the crowning of Mosiah as Nephite king (Mosiah 2–5) is said to correspond at thirty key points to standard Near Eastern coronation rituals. These include the custom of bringing precious gifts, the erection of a speaker's tower to make the king visible, a lengthy address, and the engagement of the people in choral responses.[14] But on closer inspection, some of the similarities bear only superficial resemblance and do not hold up as true parallels.

Other parallels can be explained by common circumstances. For example, the nature of any coronation event would suggest bringing gifts, while any gathering of a large crowd might inspire the building of a structure to make the speaker visible.

Latter-day Saints see significant parallels between Lehi's journey through the Middle Eastern desert (1 Nephi) and ancient Arabian practices. For example, just as Lehi fled from Jerusalem, fearing pursuit from political enemies, ancient Palestinian documents describe how wealthy people escaped Jerusalem under like circumstances. But the same action would likely occur in similar circumstances in any era or culture. The fact that Lehi lived in a tent is seen as a parallel to Middle Eastern sheikhs, for whom the tent is the center of life. But would not anyone living nomadically be likely to inhabit something like a tent? To be valid, a potential parallel must be specific enough that it cannot be explained by general human experience.[15]

Other proposed parallels are simply spurious. For instance, one LDS writer asserts that in 1 Nephi, "Lehi vividly describes a *sayl*, a flash flood of 'filthy water' out of a wadi or stream bed that can sweep one's camp away (1 Ne. 8:13; 12:16), a common event in the area where he was traveling."[16] This statement leads the reader to suppose that Lehi was describing a phenomenon common in Arabia. If so, this would connect Lehi's story with an actual place. But in fact, Lehi saw the river in a vision. Nothing in his description links the river he saw to a wadi or a flash flood in any way. To claim that "Lehi vividly describes a *sayl*" goes far beyond what the Book of Mormon text actually says to assume the conclusion that the apologist already had in mind.

A Nineteenth-Century Text?

Since its publication, observers have noted that the Book of Mormon contains numerous parallels to nineteenth-century American life. In chapter 1 I mentioned Alexander Campbell, a leading American theologian from Joseph Smith's time. In his review of the Book of Mormon, Campbell noted that Smith had written into the book "every error and almost every truth discussed in N. York for the last ten years."

He decides all the great controversies—infant baptism, ordination, the trinity, regeneration, repentance, justification, the fall of man, the atonement, transubstantiation, fasting, penance, church government, religious experience, the call to the ministry, the general resurrection, eternal punishment, who may baptize, and even the question of freemasonry, republican government, and the rights of man. All these topics are repeatedly alluded to.[17]

As Campbell observed, the Book of Mormon reflects nineteenth-century American theological and political themes. It offers guidance on democracy, the practice of capitalism, and various Protestant controversies. Some scholars see parallels between the Book of Mormon's secret societies—the Gadianton robbers—and contemporary concerns about Freemasonry. Many see the warning in 1 Nephi 13 about a "great and abominable church" as a close parallel to anti-Catholic propaganda in the 1830s.

Sermons by Nephite prophets echo the form and language of nineteenth-century evangelists. The conversion experiences described in the

Book of Mormon are similar to spiritual awakenings commonly reported in the American revival movement of the early 1800s.[18] Why are the contents of an ancient work so closely tied to the concerns of one American generation?

Battle of the Parallels

LDS scholars counter that, as a translation, the Book of Mormon can be expected to reflect the time and place in which it was translated. They recognize many of the parallels cited, but argue that instead of being unique to nineteenth-century America, these reflect universal questions of human life. Where the Book of Mormon does speak directly to particulars of Joseph Smith's environment, they assert, this is evidence of the book's prophetic power. If God intended the Book of Mormon to speak to Smith's generation, Mormons are not surprised that it addresses concrete issues from American life. From this perspective, the parallels actually confirm the prophetic accuracy of the Book of Mormon.[19]

In the end, the question is: Which parallels are more convincing? Those that link the Book of Mormon to the ancient Near East, or those that connect it to Joseph Smith's American context? Taking the evidence of archaeology, literary parallels, and nineteenth-century anachronisms all into account, people who are not already convinced of the Book of Mormon's claims have reason to doubt that it is an ancient book.

One reason faithful Latter-day Saints are convinced that the Book of Mormon is ancient scripture is the way in which the book impacts their lives. So far we have looked into the content of the Book of Mormon and evaluated some of its controversial claims. Our survey would not be complete without considering, in the next chapter, how Latter-day Saints use and experience the Book of Mormon in their daily lives.

8

THE KEYSTONE OF THE MORMON FAITH

How Do Latter-day Saints Use the Book of Mormon?

When Carma Naylor served as a Mormon missionary in New Zealand, she often heard the other missionaries testify of their certainty that the LDS Church was true and that Joseph Smith was a prophet of God. She longed for some kind of spiritual experience that would give her that same assurance.

> I was very desirous for the Lord to give me some special confirmation from the Holy Ghost concerning the truthfulness of the Book of Mormon. Each morning I read the Book of Mormon on my knees by my bedside, praying for such an experience. Finally, after several weeks, while reading the words of King Benjamin in the Book of Mormon about service and humility ... a strong emotion of warmth, goodness, and love filled me as I thought of my family back home, combined with the beautiful words from the Book of Mormon. I concluded that this love I felt was the Holy Ghost confirming to me the truthfulness of the Book of Mormon.... This was a happy sensation that tingled through me and left me feeling somewhat weak and dizzy. Because of this experience I knew the Book of Mormon was true, and I could testify accordingly. I had received the spiritual witness I had been seeking and anxiously anticipating.[1]

Latter-day Saints study the Book of Mormon to learn important lessons for their lives. The book shapes their identity and culture. But

Naylor's experience illustrates what may be the Book of Mormon's central role: it catalyzes a spiritual experience that validates Joseph Smith and the LDS Church.

"The Most Correct Book"

In chapter 1, I quoted a statement from Joseph Smith that reflects the feeling Latter-day Saints have toward the Book of Mormon: "I told the brethren that the Book of Mormon was the most correct of any book on earth, and the keystone of our religion, and a man would get nearer to God by abiding by its precepts, than by any other book."[2]

Latter-day Saints thus read the book expecting to draw closer to God and to grow in righteousness as they approach it with faith and prayer. LDS leaders encourage their members to read the book and to follow and share its teachings. Recently, President Gordon B. Hinckley challenged the LDS people to read one and a half chapters a day in order to finish the Book of Mormon by the end of the year:

> Without reservation I promise you that if each of you will observe this simple program, regardless of how many times you previously may have read the Book of Mormon, there will come into your lives and into your homes an added measure of the Spirit of the Lord, a strengthened resolution to walk in obedience to His commandments, and a stronger testimony of the living reality of the Son of God.[3]

In response to this, my sister and her family read the Book of Mormon out loud as a family every day that year.

Usually the Book of Mormon is studied individually or as a family. Some Latter-day Saints mark the pages with colored pencils or make notes in the margins. Many use study supplements available in LDS bookstores. Groups that meet informally to discuss the Book of Mormon are rare, unlike traditional Christian Bible study groups. But

© Wanda Anthony. Image from BigStockPhoto.com

Book of Mormon is a regular subject of Sunday school and seminary classes. LDS leaders do not preach from the Book of Mormon as Protestant pastors do from the Bible, although its principles inform many of their talks.

Nephi wrote that in his teaching, he "did liken the scriptures unto us, that it might be for our profit and learning" (1 Nephi 19:23). "Likening the scriptures" is a unique LDS phrase that describes how, as you read, you place yourself within the text, to see your own individual life situations in the pages of the book. Latter-day Saints have great confidence that the Book of Mormon will provide wisdom for their lives. They believe that the Book of Mormon writers foresaw the modern world and consciously included material that would speak to current times. They expect to receive the promptings of the Holy Spirit as they read. Thus a former LDS prophet, President Ezra Taft Benson, promised:

There is a power in [the Book of Mormon] which will begin to flow into your lives the moment you begin a serious study of the book. You will find greater power to resist temptation. You will find the power to avoid deception. You will find the power to stay on the strait and narrow path. The scriptures are called "the words of life" (see D&C 84:85), and nowhere is that more true than it is of the Book of Mormon. When you begin to hunger and thirst after those words, you will find life in greater and greater abundance.[4]

Shaping a Subculture

Not all Latter-day Saints study the Book of Mormon with great commitment. Even so, the book exerts a powerful, formative influence on every aspect of Mormon life. Young men are named Alma and Moroni after Book of Mormon characters. Thousands of Mormons have grown up in Utah towns with Book of Mormon names like Manti and Nephi. The book provides the plot of several grand annual pageants, which retell the story for the faithful, fortifying their roots and ideals as a people. Pageantry, in turn, fuels the widespread LDS interest in drama, music, and dance.

The Book of Mormon reinforces the "generative or founding events" that form the identity of the group and "melds them into a community."[5] It reminds them of key values, including personal revelation and modern-day prophecy. Its characters model how a testimony of spiritual truth is both gained and shared. The book's heroes and villains provide stereotypes by which the people and institutions of the world can be judged, as well as an example of foundational principles for each new generation:

> For LDS children, the Book of Mormon is a source of stories and heroes to equal those of the Bible. . . . They tell and sing with enthusiasm about the army of faithful young men led by Helaman (Alma 56:41 – 50); of the prophet Abinadi's courage before wicked King Noah (Mosiah 11 – 17); of Nephi and his unwavering faithfulness (1 Nephi 3 – 18); of Abish, a Lamanite woman

who for many years appears to be the lone believer in Christ in King Lamoni's court until the missionary Ammon taught the gospel to the king and queen (Alma 19); and of Jesus' appearances to the Nephites (3 Nephi 11–28). There are many favorites. The book is used to teach children doctrines, provide examples of the Christlike life, and remind them of God's great love and hope for all his children.[6]

The Book of Mormon's influence on LDS culture is demonstrated by the number of consumer products it has inspired. You can buy a polo shirt embroidered with the angel Moroni, or a T-shirt printed with a Book of Mormon quote. You can give your daughter a tiny Book of Mormon charm for her bracelet, while your son might enjoy a Nephi action figure. Your family can play games like "Book of Mormon Quest" or "Settlers of Zarahemla." The Book of Mormon has inspired a genre of youth fiction, a few feature films, and a whole series of animated adventure videos. Latter-day Saints use these products to declare and fortify their allegiance to the Book of Mormon and everything it represents.

Validation of the Truth

My LDS nephew and his wife tell me that the Book of Mormon's most important role is "the convincing of the Jew and Gentile that Jesus is the Christ, the Eternal God."[7] The book itself expects its readers to seek a spiritual experience that will convince them of the truth of its message and thus verify the mission of Joseph Smith. Moroni 10:4 says:

> And when ye shall receive these things, I would exhort you that ye would ask God, the Eternal Father, in the name of Christ, if these things are not true; and if ye shall ask with a sincere heart, with real intent, having faith in Christ, he will manifest the truth of it unto you, by the power of the Holy Ghost.

The book boldly invites a response — not to evaluate its ideas, doctrines, or historicity, but to ask God if it is true, with the sincere

LDS children engage their imagination with Book of Mormon action figures.

expectation that God will not fail to make its truthfulness known by supernatural means.

This invitation is directed to those who grow up within Mormonism. Young people are urged to "gain a testimony" for themselves by reading and praying about the Book of Mormon. This spiritual witness is a crucial formative experience by which those who are raised in the faith are individually converted to it. "For millions of Latter-day Saints, their most important experience with the Book of Mormon has been the spiritual knowledge that they have received of its truth."[8]

This foundational experience is reinforced frequently in LDS social life. For example, church meetings regularly feature a time when members can openly share the testimony they have gained and hear the confirming testimonies of others.

The invitation is also directed to potential converts investigating Mormonism. The Book of Mormon is the LDS Church's most important missionary tool. "All LDS missionaries encourage those they contact to read and pray about the book as a means of receiving their own testimony from God about the truthfulness of the Book of Mormon."[9]

This experience of gaining a testimony is decisive. If the Book of Mormon is accepted as divine scripture, then it is possible, even necessary, to accept Joseph Smith's spiritual authority.[10] Doubts or criticisms toward the Book of Mormon or Mormonism are resolved by an appeal to this confirming experience. Several times Latter-day Saints have told me, "It don't care what evidence you present. I just *know* the Book of Mormon is true."

How Do We Know the Truth?

In response, I believe that experience alone is an inadequate test of truth. In most cases, an experience will simply validate what we already expect it to mean. What's more, emotional experiences can be prompted by many different circumstances. The feelings that might validate the Book of Mormon are similar to feelings anyone may have at moments of family closeness or when soldiers return home. But such events do not necessarily carry spiritual or revelatory significance.

The Bible teaches us to evaluate truth by comparing truth claims to the standard of scripture. For example, 1 John 4:1–3 warns us, in the light of the prevalence of false prophets, to "test the spirits." The kind of test spelled out is not experience but comparison of doctrinal truth. Experience certainly has a role to play in the Christian life. Our spiritual experiences are part of the overall validation of our faith. Yet experience must be subservient to the revealed truth of the Bible.

Carma Naylor discovered the limitations of spiritual experience years after she completed her LDS mission. Eventually she left Mormonism to follow historic, biblical Christianity. As she reflected on her LDS testimony, she now understands what happened in a different light:

When I got that good feeling as a missionary, I was seeking a good feeling or some spiritual sign to convince me that the Book of Mormon was true.... Then, I had wanted and expected a witness of the Book of Mormon so I could testify that I knew it was true. That is what I was sent out to do as a missionary. The pressure was on me to say, "I know the Book of Mormon is true and that Joseph Smith was a true prophet." Now, however ... I was committed to God's truth only, rather than committed to my church and to being a good missionary. That had made all the difference![11]

If you ever have an opportunity to talk to an LDS friend about the Book of Mormon, your friend will most likely invite you to read the book and even pray for a testimony about it. Should you read the Book of Mormon? How should you discuss it with Latter-day Saints? You've gained a lot of insight about the Book of Mormon as you've read this book. Now, in chapter 9, let me give you some advice about how to talk with your LDS acquaintances about what you've learned.

9

WITH GENTLENESS AND RESPECT

How Do We Talk to Latter-day Saints
about the Book of Mormon?

I asked my LDS family members to help me prepare for this book by
sharing their experiences and perspectives about the Book of Mormon. With those who were willing, I had some delightful and informative discussions. But when I started to touch on controversial issues, even gently, the conversation was doused. All of us are protective of our cherished beliefs.

But Latter-day Saints also have a history of being persecuted and criticized, along with a consciousness of being different. As your knowledge of the Book of Mormon grows, you may have an opportunity to talk to your LDS acquaintances about it. This may lead to an opportunity to share your faith in Christ. How you handle that conversation will either open doors of communication or erect walls between you and your Mormon visitors.

The Basic Options

Let's begin by reviewing some of the evidence we have looked at throughout this book to see where it leads. Keep in mind that different assumptions lead to different interpretations of the evidence, which result in different conclusions about the Book of Mormon.[1] As we have seen, most Latter-day Saints believe that the Book of Mormon is divinely inspired scripture, an ancient record given to Joseph Smith by the angel Moroni to translate by the gift and power of God. They find it unlikely that the uneducated Smith could have written a book with the complexity and inner consistency of the Book of Mormon. They cite the testimony of reliable witnesses who claimed to see and touch the gold plates. They list parallels between the Book of Mormon and ancient Near Eastern language and culture that suggest an ancient origin for the book. They see the growth and vibrancy of Mormonism as a validation of the entire story of Joseph Smith.

Joseph Smith

Another school of thought is that Smith composed the Book of Mormon himself, drawing on contemporary literary sources. Those who hold this view point to the book's significant parallels with nineteenth century American themes and issues. They note the changes and inconsistencies in Smith's accounts of his visions, along with the magic worldview and practices from which the story sprang. They observe the Book of Mormon's apparent dependence on the King James Version of the Bible, as well as the lack of archaeological evidence for the Book of Mormon. They point to Smith's native imagination and ingenuity and to the visionary history of his family to explain how he could have written the book. Some even suggest that he had help from an unknown source. If Smith wrote the Book of Mormon himself, some imply from this that he was a charlatan. But others point out that he could have truly believed his composition to be from God, or he could have written it with pious motives.

A third theory is that Smith wrote the Book of Mormon unconsciously or unintentionally, in some state of psychological dissociation. Various writers suggest different angles on this view: either Smith had hallucinations induced by epilepsy, or he ingested psychoactive plants, or he worked under some form of hypnotic suggestion, or some type of "automatic writing" arose from his subconscious mind.[2] One problem with this approach is the great difficulty in assessing anyone's frame of mind or inner life from a distance of almost two hundred years. The varying theories show how subjective is the psychobiography approach to Book of Mormon authorship.[3]

Another view is that Smith wrote or received the Book of Mormon as the product of direct demonic deception. The Bible allows for the possibility that Satan disguises himself as an "angel of light" in order to deceive (2 Corinthians 11:13–15). If Smith himself was genuinely deceived, he passed on to his followers what he sincerely but falsely believed was true. But theories of hallucinations or false visions fail to take into account physical evidence. For example, many people reported feeling an object as it lay in the Smith home under a cloth, or picking it up while covered by a cloth.[4] Apparently some actual artifact existed—either gold plates dug by Smith from the Hill Cumorah or some kind of replica created by him to sustain his story. If so, this supports either those who believe the Book of Mormon is true or those who see it as a conscious fabrication of Joseph Smith.

Handling Disagreement

People who hold different views of the Book of Mormon often have difficulty talking to each other. Given its significance to so many people along with the controversy over its nature and origin, conversations about the Book of Mormon can become emotionally heated. That doesn't have to be the case.

Remember that for your LDS friend, the ultimate evidence for the Book of Mormon is a spiritual experience. All the other lines of argument merely confirm what Mormons claim to know by direct revelation. Don't get frustrated when the points you make don't seem to get through. Your friend may quickly disregard what you think is a strong argument, simply because Latter-day Saints give the ultimate weight to their personal testimony. Moreover, most Mormons are not aware of, or have not reflected on, the kind of issues you have been introduced to in this book.

In fact, I don't believe most Mormons want to know or think about these issues. In my experience, the greatest fear of a faithful Latter-day Saint is to fall into apostasy. Mormons protect their testimony against what they consider the upsetting prospect that they could lose it. So if your LDS friend disregards your arguments, it may be in part because they make him or her feel vulnerable. Handle these controversial subjects delicately.

Don't forget how meaningful the Book of Mormon is for Latter-day Saints. The book is at the heart of their identity and culture. They value its stories and principles, honor its heroes, cherish its portrayal of Jesus Christ, and find encouragement in its promises of salvation and personal revelation. You may not see your comments as an assault on the Book of Mormon, but your LDS friend very well might. After all, think about how you feel when someone challenges beliefs that you hold dear.

The Mormons were threatened and mistreated frequently throughout their early history. Even today, Latter-day Saints feel persecuted when critics misrepresent their beliefs and practices, or when they present a sensationalized view of Mormonism. Thus, when you or I speak to a Latter-day Saint about their faith, they expect to be condemned and to have their views belittled. Perhaps Latter-day Saints are too quick to become defensive when others disagree. But understanding their suspicions makes it even more important to follow the counsel of 1 Peter 3:15: "Always be prepared to give an answer to everyone who asks you to give the reason for the hope that you have. But do this with gentleness and respect."

As this verse suggests, we pray that our LDS friends might have an opportunity to understand the hope in Jesus that we have. Yet traditional Christians disagree with Latter-day Saints on many fundamental issues, such as the authority of the Bible, the nature of God, and the meaning of salvation. Even so, we can share our perspective with respect by seeking to truly understand their viewpoint, by avoiding inflammatory language, and by never mocking what they hold dear. We can share with gentleness by stating our views with humility and without anger and by trying to avoid unnecessary offense. This kind of civility builds trust, making it more likely that you will genuinely understand your LDS friends and they will actually hear what you say.

Sensitivity about Smith

Latter-day Saints use the Book of Mormon to establish the authority of Joseph Smith. But conversely, Smith's credibility also affects how we view the validity of the Book of Mormon. If this is so, you will want to know about three particular issues. The first is Smith's performance as a prophet. According to Deuteronomy 18:21–22, a prophet can be tested by whether his prophecies come true. Several of Smith's specific predictions have failed to happen, casting doubt on whether he actually spoke for God.[5]

The second issue is Smith's track record as a translator. His translation of the Book of Abraham does not match the Egyptian papyrus from which it was derived. On another occasion, Smith was presented with metal plates etched with unrecognizable characters, known as the Kinderhook plates. They were fraudulent, but Smith did not recognize this. People close to him reported that he actually began to translate them.[6]

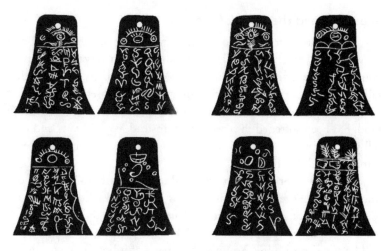

Some of the Kinderhook plates

Originally published in *The Nauvoo Neighbor*, June 1843.

A third problem area is Smith's covert practice of polygamy. He reportedly received a revelation (D&C 132) commanding him to practice plural marriage. On this basis, he secretly married as many as thirty-three women, including several who were already married to other men at the time. All the while, Smith was officially denying any association with the practice. The revelation was not made public until after Smith's death — when the Mormons had settled in Utah.[7]

Yet I would not be too quick to raise these issues with an LDS friend. Mormons have strong feelings of reverence and admiration for Joseph Smith as an inspired leader, an anointed prophet of God, and a courageous martyr for Christ. If you criticize Smith, they will feel attacked. I would discuss the problems with Joseph Smith only when the relationship has developed a high level of rapport and trust — and even then, only with great caution.

Should I Read the Book of Mormon?

If you enter into discussion with a Latter-day Saint about the Book of Mormon, you should realize that your friend will want to convert you. The large majority of converts to Mormonism come from other faiths, mostly Christian. The strident approach of Joseph Smith's First Vision, which declared all Christian creeds to be an abomination to God, has been softened in recent years. Instead, your LDS friend may tell you that while your faith is good, you can have so much more by joining the LDS Church.

Don't be surprised if you are asked to read the Book of Mormon. Your friend believes that this is the most effective way to convert you. What should you do? I don't see any harm in reading the Book of Mormon if you evaluate it from a sound biblical perspective as you go. It will be time-consuming. You may find parts of it boring or confusing. But reading the book is a good way to engage your friend in conversation about spiritual truth, with the hope that it may open doors for you to share your faith in Jesus. If you do read it, insist that your friend discuss it with you and answer your questions along the way. Or you may agree to read the Book of Mormon if your friend will read the New Testament and talk with you about it every few chapters. Start with Romans or John, and use a modern translation.

The Latter-day Saints also encourage prospective converts to pray about the Book of Mormon. I don't recommend that you go that far. There's no need to ask God to show you whether it is true. While you and I do pray for guidance in every area of life, we have seen that the ultimate test of truth is not a spiritual experience. A Latter-day Saint would not accept an invitation to pray for a testimony of the Koran (the holy book of the Islamic faith), because he or she will already feel confident about knowing the truth. In the same way, it's fair for you to decline to pray about the Book of Mormon.

Before my father passed away, he urged me to pray once more about the truth of Mormonism and implored me to return to the LDS Church. I respectfully told him that I didn't need to pray about it. The truth has been tested and confirmed to me in many ways over the thirty-plus years I've followed Jesus since leaving Mormonism. I know my father only wanted what he felt was best for me. But to accept his invitation to pray about Mormonism would be to deny everything God has done in my life and everything I have already established to be true.

Some Concluding Words to the Reader

The claims that Latter-day Saints make for the Book of Mormon are serious and far-reaching. I believe that the burden of proof is on those who make such claims rather than on those who question them. As we have seen, there are good reasons to question. Much of the evidence is persuasive only to those who are already committed to Joseph Smith as a prophet. But even though we don't accept the Book of Mormon as an ancient scripture, we still recognize how deeply important the book is to Latter-day Saints.

As I pass on what I've learned about the Book of Mormon to you, my hope is that you will be prepared to talk to your Mormon neighbors and friends when opportunities arise. I pray that the Holy Spirit will enable you to express the truth with gentleness and respect. I've seen many Latter-day Saints come to discover a life-changing faith in Jesus Christ through the support and encouragement of Christian friends. This is what happened in my own life. Of course, only God can change anyone's heart. But he uses people to reach people. So my prayer is that God will use you to help others discover the truth, as you graciously share with them the insights you have learned.

DISCUSSION QUESTIONS

CHAPTER 1

1. In what ways have you observed Mormonism in the news or media recently? What is your impression of the LDS Church based on what you've seen?

2. Have you known any Latter-day Saints personally? What traits or qualities come to mind when you think of those individuals?

3. What did you know about the Book of Mormon before you read this chapter? What did you know about Joseph Smith? Has your perception changed? If so, in what ways?

4. How do you respond to the LDS claim that original Christianity fell into apostasy and foundational truths were lost? What evidence from history and from contemporary Christianity might support that view? What evidence from the Bible and history refutes it?

5. In this chapter, former LDS Church President Gordon B. Hinckley is quoted as saying: "I cannot understand why the Christian world does not accept this book." What are some reasons why the Christian world does not embrace the Book of Mormon?

CHAPTER 2

1. Reconstruct the basic story line of the Book of Mormon in its major movements. How does the story begin? How does it end? What are the major occurrences in between?

2. What do you find intriguing about the Book of Mormon's

story? Why? What do you find difficult to believe? Why?

3. What are the major traits of the Nephite people? Of the Lamanite people? Of the Jaredite people? What do you think about the idea that righteous Lamanites became like the Nephites?

4. What elements of the Book of Mormon's story are similar to the Bible? What elements are different from the Bible?

5. The centerpiece of the Book of Mormon's story is the appearance of Jesus in the Americas. Does this seem plausible to you? Why or why not?

CHAPTER 3

1. The author writes, "Traditional Christians have no problem, in principle, with the appearance of an angel to a prophet or with the revelation of divine scripture." Do you agree or disagree? Why?

2. If someone today claimed to receive divine revelation, how should we test that claim?

3. Review the section in the chapter that describes the Smith family's spiritual search. How was their journey different from your own spiritual journey? In your opinion, where did they miss the mark?

4. Latter-day Saints offer several lines of evidence to support the idea that Joseph Smith did not write the Book of Mormon but received it from God. What are they? Which of these points do you find the strongest or most difficult to refute?

5. What do you find to be the strongest points of evidence against the LDS claims about the origin of the Book of Mormon?

CHAPTER 4

1. What was your reaction when you learned that the Book of Mormon is filled with references to Jesus? In your opinion, how biblical is the Book of Mormon's portrayal of Jesus?

2. According to the author, "The Bible teaches that there is only one God, who exists eternally in three persons: Father, Son, and Holy Spirit." What biblical references can you think of to support the teaching that there is only one God? How would you support the deity of Jesus and of the Holy Spirit?

3. The author states that "the Bible teaches that human beings were created good, but disobeyed God and thus fell into a darkened moral condition marked by sin." Where would you look in the Bible to support this idea?

4. How is the Book of Mormon's view of salvation similar to and different from the biblical teaching? Why do you suppose many people find it difficult to accept the idea of salvation purely as a gift of grace?

5. The author asserts that it is fruitless to argue "about who is or isn't a Christian." Why does he make that claim? Do you agree or disagree? Why? How could that approach be abused?

CHAPTER 5

1. How do you evaluate the LDS idea that many ancient books of scripture will one day be made available? If a book claiming to be scripture was unearthed, how would we put it to the test?

2. The author writes, "Historically, Christians have seen the Bible alone as God's final, authoritative word to humanity." If so, then what place does the Bible deserve in our lives? In what ways do you treat the Bible as authoritative in your life?

3. What are some of the dangers of placing the words of a living prophet over the authority of written scripture?

4. The author speaks of "religious leaders who have tried to undermine the Bible's unique authority" in order to introduce their own claims to spiritual truth. Give some historic or contemporary examples.

5. What are some unique doctrines of the LDS Church that derive from the books of Moses and Abraham, or from the Doctrine and Covenants? Can you offer a biblical response to these unique teachings?

CHAPTER 6

1. Discuss the status the Bible has in LDS thinking. In what ways does Mormonism have a low view of the Bible?

2. In what ways do Latter-day Saints have a high view of the Bible? Do you believe the Book of Mormon corroborates the Bible's message? Why or why not?

3. How do you respond to the LDS claim that the Bible is corrupted? What evidence can we offer that the Bible is, in fact, reliable?

4. Consider the Bible passages that Latter-day Saints believe are about the Book of Mormon. Read them again, trying to put yourself in a Mormon person's shoes. Can you see reasons why that person would think these passages are talking about the Book of Mormon? Discuss the reasons.

5. Summarize and discuss the evidence that suggests that the Book of Mormon borrowed heavily from the Bible. If this is the case, why would it be a problem?

CHAPTER 7

1. Which arguments against an ancient origin for the Book of Mormon do you find most convincing? Why? How might a Latter-day Saint respond to those arguments?

2. Which arguments for an ancient origin for the Book of Mormon do you think Mormons might believe to be the strongest? Why?

3. Can you explain what chiasm is? Why do Latter-day Saints believe chiasm proves an ancient origin for the Book of Mormon? What do you think about this?

4. How do the evidences for the Book of Mormon compare to the evidences for the Bible? Give some examples.

5. Some Latter-day Saints believe that the Book of Mormon is a product of the nineteenth century rather than an ancient work, but that it is still divinely inspired scripture. What is the appeal of this position? What are its weaknesses?

CHAPTER 8

1. In what ways is the role of the Book of Mormon in LDS life similar to the role the Bible plays in your life?

2. The author describes how the Book of Mormon characters provide "an example of foundational principles for each new generation." What Bible characters reinforce your values as a Christian?

3. Explain how Latter-day Saints "gain a testimony" of the truthfulness of Mormonism. Do traditional Christians have a similar experience?

4. What is the role of personal experience in the Christian life? Give some biblical examples. How is this similar to or different from the role of experience in Mormonism?

5. What are some reasons why personal experience is inadequate as an ultimate test of truth?

CHAPTER 9

1. Have you ever had opportunity to talk about matters of faith with a Mormon? What happened? What did you learn?

2. How does the LDS history of being persecuted and criticized affect how they interact with others about their beliefs? Can you think of a time when your Christian beliefs were challenged? How did you respond emotionally to that incident?

3. Is there ever a good reason to read the Book of Mormon? If so, what might it be? If you ever do read the Book of Mormon, what precautions should you take?

4. How does it make you feel to know that your LDS friend would like to see you leave your church to join Mormonism? Do you believe that Mormons should convert to a more biblical type of faith? Why or why not?

5. The author states that he would not be too quick to raise problem issues about Joseph Smith with an LDS friend. Why does he state this? Do you agree or disagree? Why?

NOTES

CHAPTER 1: THE GOLD BIBLE

1. On Book of Mormon distribution, see "Taking the Scriptures to the World," *Ensign* (July 2001), 24; and *Deseret News 2001–2002 Church Almanac* (Salt Lake City: Deseret News, 2000), 568.

2. "Book of Mormon," *The Commandments: Study the Scriptures, The Church of Jesus Christ of Latter-day Saints: Truth Restored*: www.mormon.org (accessed August 25, 2007).

3. *Book of Mormon*. (Salt Lake City: Corporation of the President of The Church of Jesus Christ of Latter-day Saints, 1981), "Introduction."

4. Ibid.

5. *Book of Mormon*, Mormon 9:32.

6. *Book of Mormon*, "Introduction."

7. Joseph Smith, *History of the Church of Jesus Christ of Latter-day Saints*, 7 vols., 2nd ed. rev. (Salt Lake City: Deseret Books, 1966), 4:461.

8. *The Pearl of Great Price* (Salt Lake City: The Church of Jesus Christ of Latter-day Saints, 1982), 52.

9. Mark Twain, *Roughing It* (New York: Signet Classic, 1962), 102.

10. Alexander Campbell, "Delusions," *The Restoration Movement Pages*, www.mun.ca/rels/restmov/people/acampbell.html (accessed August 25, 2007).

11. Susan Easton Black, *Stories from the Early Saints: Converted by the Book of Mormon* (Salt Lake City: Bookcraft, 1992), 64.

12. David E. Sorensen, "Where Is Your Book of Mormon?" *New Era* (February 2007), 47.

13. Gordon B. Hinckley, "The Marvelous Foundation of Our Faith," *Ensign* (November 2002), 81.

CHAPTER 3: THE MYSTERIOUS ORIGIN OF
THE BOOK OF MORMON

1. For basic biographical information, I mainly rely on Richard L. Bushman, *Joseph Smith: Rough Stone Rolling* (New York: Vintage, 2005).

2. On the role of folk magic and occult practices in Smith's family and cultural environment, see D. Michael Quinn, *Early Mormonism and the Magic World View*, rev. and enlarged ed. (Salt Lake City: Signature, 1998), 30–65.

3. The story is told in "Joseph Smith—History 1:7–20" in *The Pearl of Great Price*, 48–50.

4. On the different accounts of the First Vision, see LaMar Peterson, *The Creation of the Book of Mormon: A Historical Inquiry* (Salt Lake City: Freethinker Press, 1998), 1–10.

5. Bushman, *Joseph Smith*, 39–40.

6. The story of Moroni's appearances to Smith and his receiving the gold plates is found in "Joseph Smith—History 1:27–59" in *The Pearl of Great Price*, 51–56.

7. On the translation process, see James E. Lancaster, "The Translation of the Book of Mormon," *The Word of God: Essays on Mormon Scripture*, ed. Dan Vogel (Salt Lake City: Signature, 1990), 97–112.

8. An LDS evaluation of the theories that ascribe authorship to Joseph Smith is found in Terryl L. Givens, *By the Hand of Mormon: The American Scripture That Launched a New World Religion* (New York: Oxford Univ. Press, 2002), 155–84.

9. More information about Smith's activity as a money-digger is found in H. Michael Marquardt, *The Rise of Mormonism: 1816–1844* (Longwood, FL: Xulon, 2005), 53–76.

10. "Joseph Smith—History 1:28," in *The Pearl of Great Price*, 51.

11. Bushman, *Joseph Smith*, 73.

12. For an overview of these accounts, see Cameron J. Parker, "Cumorah's Cave," *Journal of Book of Mormon Studies* 13, no. 1–2 (2004): 50–57.

13. *Book of Mormon*, "Introduction."

14. On the witnesses, see Dan Vogel, "The Validity of the Witnesses' Testimonies," *American Apocrypha: Essays on the Book of Mormon*, ed. Dan Vogel and Brent Lee Metcalfe (Salt Lake City: Signature, 2002), 79–121.

15. For an LDS response to critiques of the Book of Mormon witnesses, see Givens, *By the Hand of Mormon*, 37–42.

16. These parallels will be outlined in ch. 7.

17. On Smith's qualifications for authorship, see Fawn M. Brodie, *No Man Knows My History*, 2nd ed. (New York: Vintage, 1995), 35, 67–73.

18. This subjective, inner testimony of the Book of Mormon will be discussed in ch. 8.

CHAPTER 4: THE FULLNESS OF THE EVERLASTING GOSPEL?

1. "Joseph Smith—History 1:34" in *The Pearl of Great Price*, 52.

2. 2 Nephi 2:14; 11:5; Jacob 4:5; 3 Nephi 19:7.

3. 2 Nephi 26:13; 31:12; Jacob 7:12; Moroni 6:9.

4. Dallin H. Oaks, "Apostasy and Restoration," *Ensign* (May 1995), 84.

5. *Book of Mormon Student Manual: Religion 121 and 122* (Church Educational System; Salt Lake City: Church of Jesus Christ of Latter-day Saints, 1996), 63.

6. Joseph Smith Jr., "The King Follett Sermon," *Ensign* (April 1971), 13–17. Smith said, speaking of God the Father, "He was once a man like us; yea, that God himself, the Father of us all, dwelt on an earth."

7. Ida Smith, "The Lord as a Role Model for Men and Women," *Ensign* (August 1980), 66.

8. Gayle Oblad Brown, "Premortal Life," in *Encyclopedia of Mormonism*, ed. Daniel H. Ludlow (New York: Macmillan, 1992), 1123.

9. See "Exaltation," ch. 47 in *Gospel Principles* (Salt Lake City: Church of Jesus Christ of Latter-day Saints, 1997), 301–2.

10. *The Doctrine and Covenants* (Salt Lake City: Church of Jesus Christ of Latter-day Saints, 1982), sec. 76:49–93, esp. vv. 71–81. This book of LDS scripture is commonly abbreviated as D&C.

11. In the King Follett sermon, Smith said, "You have got to learn how to be gods yourselves, and to be kings and priests to God, the same as all gods have done before you" (*Ensign* [April 1971], 16).

12. D&C 132:19–21.

13. D&C 138:32–34, 58–59.

14. 1 Nephi 16:24–31; Jacob 2:11; Alma 16:5–6; 40:9; 43:23. For a discussion of personal revelation in the Book of Mormon, see Givens, *By the Hand of Mormon*, 221–26.

CHAPTER 5: NEW SCRIPTURES FOR THE LAST DAYS

1. "The Articles of Faith 9" in *The Pearl of Great Price*, 60.

2. *Gospel Principles*, 52.

3. W. D. Davies and Truman G. Madsen, "Scripture," in *Encyclopedia of Mormonism*, 1278.

4. "Explanatory Introduction" in *The Doctrine and Covenants*.

5. For introductory information about the D&C and its contents, see Roy W. Doxey et al. "Doctrine and Covenants," in *Encyclopedia of Mormonism*, 404–24.

6. For an overview of the Book of Moses, see Bruce T. Taylor, "Book of Moses," in *Encyclopedia of Mormonism*. 216–17; Bushman, *Joseph Smith*, 132–42.

7. *The Pearl of Great Price*, 29.

8. On the origin and contents of the Book of Abraham, see H. Donl Peterson, Stephen E. Thompson, and Michael D. Rhodes, "Book of Abraham," in *Encyclopedia of Mormonism*, 132–38; also Bushman, *Joseph Smith*, 285–90.

9. For a thorough treatment of the problems raised by the rediscovery of the Book of Abraham scrolls, see Charles M. Larson, *By His Own Hand upon Papyrus*, rev. ed. (Grand Rapids, MI: Institute for Religious Research, 1992).

10. Bushman, *Joseph Smith*, 291–92.

11. For an introduction to the Inspired Version of the Bible, see Robert J. Matthews, "Joseph Smith Translation of the Bible," in *Encyclopedia of Mormonism*, 763–69; Bushman, *Joseph Smith*, 132, 142. For a critique of the Inspired Version, see Jerald and Sandra Tanner. *Mormonism—Shadow or Reality?* enlarged ed. (Salt Lake City: Modern Microfilm, 1972), 386–97.

CHAPTER 6: ANOTHER TESTAMENT OF JESUS CHRIST

1. For example, compare 1 Nephi 20–21 to Isaiah 48–49; 2 Nephi 7–8 to Isaiah 50–51; and 2 Nephi 12–24 to Isaiah 2–14.

2. Givens, *By the Hand of Mormon*, 186–87.

3. This twofold relationship is discussed in Givens, ibid., 188–94.

4. "Articles of Faith," in *The Pearl of Great Price*, 60.

5. To understand the transmission of the Bible, see Bruce M. Metzger, *The Text of the New Testament* (London: Oxford Univ. Press, 1964.)

6. These various types of parallels are described in Mark D. Thomas, "Scholarship and the Book of Mormon," in *The Word of God: Essays on Mormon Scripture*, 68.

7. Givens, *By the Hand of Mormon*, 49.

8. "A Brief Explanation about the Book of Mormon," in the *Book of Mormon*.

9. For details about issues in the Book of Mormon's use of Isaiah, see David P. Wright, "Isaiah in the Book of Mormon: Or Joseph Smith in Isaiah," in *American Apocrypha: Essays on the Book of Mormon*, 169–82.

CHAPTER 7: SEARCH FOR A MISSING CIVILIZATION

1. The most widely accepted attempt to correlate the Book of Mormon with Mesoamerican geography and culture is John L. Sorenson, *An Ancient American Setting for the Book of Mormon* (Salt Lake City: Deseret Book and FARMS, 1985).

2. David J. Johnson, "Archaeology," *Encyclopedia of Mormonism*, 62–63.

3. On the use of metals in Mesoamerica, see Deanne G. Matheny, "Does the Shoe Fit? A Critique of the Limited Tehauntepec Geography," *American Apocrypha: Essays on the Book of Mormon*, 283–97.

4. On crops and animals, see ibid., 302–10.

5. On the archaeological confirmation of the Bible, see Joseph P. Free, *Archaeology and Bible History,* revised and expanded by Howard F. Vos (Grand Rapids: Zondervan, 1992).

6. On the DNA issue, see D. Jeffrey Meldrum and Trent D. Stephens, "Who Are the Children of Lehi?" *Journal of Book of Mormon Studies* 12, no. 1 (2003): 38–51.

7. Carrie A. Moore, "Debate Renewed with Change of Book of Mormon Introduction," *The Deseret Morning News* (November 8, 2007).

8. D. Brent Anderson and Diane E. Wirth introduce the claim of Near Eastern parallels in "Book of Mormon Authorship," *Encyclopedia of Mormonism*, 166–67.

9. Hugh W. Nibley, "Book of Mormon Near Eastern Background," *Encyclopedia of Mormonism*, 187.

10. The case for chiasm is made by John W. Welch, "Chiasmus in the Book of Mormon," *Book of Mormon Authorship: New Light on Ancient Origins*, ed. Noel B. Reynolds. (Provo, UT: Religious Study Center, Brigham Young University, 1982), 33–52.

11. Givens, *By the Hand of Mormon*, 140–41.

12. Thomas J. Finley evaluates the claim of ancient Near Eastern names in the Book of Mormon in "Does the Book of Mormon Reflect an Ancient Near Eastern Background?" *The New Mormon Challenge*, ed. Francis J. Beckwith, Carl Mosser, and Paul Owen (Grand Rapids: Zondervan, 2002), 353–59. Finley also responds to other LDS claims of Hebraisms in the Book of Mormon.

13. Edward H. Ashment, "'A Record in the Language of My Father': Evidence of Ancient Egyptian and Hebrew in the Book of Mormon," *New Approaches to the Book of Mormon*, ed. Brent Lee Metcalfe (Salt Lake City: Signature, 1993), 375–80.

14. Givens, *By the Hand of Mormon*, 123–24.

15. A set of guidelines to weigh the validity of purported parallels is found in Finley, "Does the Book of Mormon Reflect an Ancient Near Eastern Background?" 338–39.

16. Hugh W. Nibley, "Book of Mormon Near Eastern Background," 188.

17. Alexander Campbell, "Delusions," *The Restoration Movement Pages:* http://www.mun.ca/rels/restmov/people/acampbell.html (January 4, 2008).

18. On various parallels between the Book of Mormon and nineteenth-century American life, see Mark D. Thomas, "Scholarship and the Book of Mormon," and Susan Curtis, "Early Nineteenth-Century America and the Book of Mormon," in *The Word of God: Essays on Mormon Scripture* (Salt Lake City: Signature, 1990), 63–79, 81–96. On parallels to revivalist conversion and preaching, see Grant Palmer, *An Insider's View of Mormon Origins* (Salt Lake City: Signature, 2002), 95–133. On the background of Freemasonry, see Dan Vogel, "Echoes of Anti-Masonry: A Rejoinder to Critics of the Anti-Masonic Thesis," *American Apocrypha: Essays on the Book of Mormon*, ed. Dan Vogel and Brent Lee Metcalfe (Salt Lake City: Signature, 2002), 275–320.

19. A thoughtful LDS perspective on the nineteenth-century parallels is found in Givens, *By the Hand of Mormon,* 165–67.

CHAPTER 8: THE KEYSTONE OF THE MORMON FAITH

1. Carma Naylor, *A Mormon's Unexpected Journey,* vol. 1. (Enumclaw, WA: Winepress, 2006), 11–12.

2. Smith, *History of the Church of Jesus Christ of Latter-day Saints*, 4:461.

3. Gordon B. Hinckley, "A Testimony Vibrant and True," *Ensign* (August 2005), 6.

4. Ezra Taft Benson, "The Book of Mormon—Keystone of Our Religion," *Ensign* (November 1986), 7.

5. Louis Midgley. "To Remember and Keep," *The Disciple as Scholar: Essays on Scripture and the Ancient World*, ed. Stephen D. Ricks, Donald W.

Parry, and Andrew H. Hedges (Provo, UT: The Foundation for Ancient Research and Mormon Studies, 2000), 103.

6. Monte S. Nyman and Lisa Bolin Hawkins, "Book of Mormon: Overview," *Encyclopedia of Mormonism*, 141. This article provides a helpful overview of many of the ways the Book of Mormon is used in LDS life.

7. *Book of Mormon*, title page.

8. Nyman and Hawkins, "Book of Mormon: Overview," 143.

9. Ibid., 142.

10. For a discussion of the how the Book of Mormon functions as a sign validating Joseph Smith's work, see Givens, *By the Hand of Mormon*, 135–38.

11. Naylor, *A Mormon's Unexpected Journey*, 240–41.

CHAPTER 9: WITH GENTLENESS AND RESPECT

1. Most of these views are discussed in Stephen D. Ricks, "Book of Mormon Studies," *Encyclopedia of Mormonism*, 209.

2. For an example of this approach, see Scott C. Dunn, "Automaticity and the Dictation of the Book of Mormon," *American Apocrypha: Essays on the Book of Mormon*, 17–46.

3. Psychobiography is the attempt to understand historically significant individuals through the application of psychological theory and research, as in Robert D. Anderson, *Inside the Mind of Joseph Smith: Psychobiography and the Book of Mormon* (Salt Lake City: Signature, 1999).

4. Bushman, *Joseph Smith*: 58–61.

5. Jerald and Sandra Tanner, *The Case against Mormonism*, vol. 3 (Salt Lake City: Modern Microfilm, 1971), 129–42.

6. Palmer, *An Insider's View of Mormon Origins*, 30–34.

7. Bushman, *Joseph Smith*: 437–41, 490–95.

SCRIPTURE INDEX

BOOK OF MORMON INDEX

SUBJECT INDEX

Share Your Thoughts

With the Author: Your comments will be forwarded to
the author when you send them to *zauthor@zondervan.com*.

With Zondervan: Submit your review of this book
by writing to *zreview@zondervan.com*.

Free Online Resources at
www.zondervan.com

Zondervan AuthorTracker: Be notified whenever your
favorite authors publish new books, go on tour, or post
an update about what's happening in their lives.

Daily Bible Verses and Devotions: Enrich your life
with daily Bible verses or devotions that help you start
every morning focused on God.

Free Email Publications: Sign up for newsletters on
fiction, Christian living, church ministry, parenting, and
more.

Zondervan Bible Search: Find and compare
Bible passages in a variety of translations at
www.zondervanbiblesearch.com.

Other Benefits: Register yourself to receive online
benefits like coupons and special offers, or to participate
in research.

ZONDERVAN®
.com